ISBN 978-0-692-56860-6
ISBN 0-069-256860-3

THE FAMILY GUIDE TO GHOST HUNTING

DAVID BRYAN LAWRENCE
WITH
CHRISTIAN LAWRENCE

Dedicated to my son, my loved ones and to my
UPST Family with love!

THE FAMILY GUIDE TO GHOST HUNTING

Table of Contents

*"If you have a something you would like
me to tell to your children, I see them every day."*

I held my breath for a moment as a light drizzle spat down
upon my team, invisible within the dark of the cemetery.
Standing motionless, I again addressed the friend's
tombstone in front of me.

"If you have a message, the time to tell me is now."

Suddenly, a response, all around us the wind and rain filled
the trees with something that was strange and magical, and
far more than a moan.

– Riverside Cemetery Investigation, 12:24 am

Foreword

This book is not meant to be read in one sitting and tossed into the closet. If you find it engrossing enough to finish today, you are surely the next coming of the ultimate paranormal investigator and I love you. In all seriousness, this book is meant to be addressed before and after every investigation, and in starting a family group. When you read the book, feel free to jump around to the Glossarex, appendixes, etc. This will aid you in sifting through the information pertinent to your team before you sit down to digest the book in its entirety.

At times, you will see me reference something to be "explained in a following chapter." When I do so, I recommend that you go directly to the Glossarex (glossary/index) for some quick info and then back to where you left off. I've also incorporated *"Christian Notes"* or *"CN:"* within the case study section of the book. They relate my son's "kid perspective" of paranormal from age four to twelve. I recommend a yellow highlighter to score important passages, or perhaps a pink one. Whatever your instrument of choice, this book is meant to be marked up!

After you have completed *The Family Guide to Ghost Hunting*, I hope you will have found PASS, the appendixes, the computer links and the team tools will forever aid your paranormal investigation endeavors. Have a great hunt!

David Lawrence

"Did you hear that?" asked Bongo as she pointed the flashlight toward the trees.

The mist swirled between the trail and the forest that adjoined it. The night was chilly, but the sheer excitement of the hunt was enough to keep the Upper Peninsula Spook Team warm. Retaining our composure, we continued our preliminary EVP session.

Zippo continued the EVP work, "If someone is there please let us know now."

The EMF (electro magnetic field) detector suddenly screeched into action producing a multitude of beeps that quickly turned into one long squeal.

– Paulding Light I Investigation, 9:47 pm

1

Ghost Hunting for Dummies
- an Introduction

So you want to be a ghost hunter, and why not?...don't worry, no one is a dummy. Paranormal investigation is one of the fastest growing hobbies in the country and is reasonably inexpensive, usually only requiring you to pay for the necessary gas to get you to a cemetery, dilapidated house, or other haunted spot. No one is a "Dummy" for wanting to pursue the paranormal and if they are I am the biggest. The equipment is not as pricy as you may believe, and I will outline the necessities in following chapters. I realize that there are a hundred paperbacks out there telling you all about paranormal investigating, but this book is different. This book is for regular people who want to learn. Everyone feels a little uncomfortable when we take on a

1

new hobby. I have always enjoyed those "For Dummies" books because they were complete and understandable. I hope I have created the same atmosphere in this book for you. What you will find of interest in the following manifesto is the "family" angle, a direction taken by few paranormal squads. I have introduced youth to our team which is viewed by some as risky, while lauded by others as genius. Excuse me if I am partial to the latter assessment...LOL! I will also delve into team make-up in later chapters, but we have many miles to go before then, so read on.

First, let me tell you about the formation of the UPST. My name is David Lawrence and I am the founder of the Upper Peninsula Spook Team (U.P.S.T). We are based in Michigan's beautiful Upper Peninsula. The Upper Peninsula - or U.P. as we call it - is an unusual place, not quite an island, but surrounded by the Great Lakes, which is the largest collection of freshwater in the world. Lake Superior on our northern shore is also the biggest freshwater lake in the world by area, and larger than the Indian Ocean. To our south is Lake Michigan and to our east Lake Huron. Lakes Eerie and Ontario fill out the five. In fact, the UP is attached to the mainland of Michigan by a five mile long suspension bridge called the Mackinac. It gives the "down-staters" or "Trolls" as we call them (from beneath the bridge... get it?) a retreat from the bustle of the bigger cities like Detroit and Grand Rapids. If water, shipwrecks and lighthouses are to paranormal investigation what condiments are to hamburgers, with 1,790 miles of lakeshore, we have ketchup and relish squirting out of our Upper Peninsula pants.

I was brought up in a family that for generations had adhered to devout Catholicism. Those of you that are Catholic understand the mysticism involved with even the most simple of life experiences. Fortunately, my parents, both educators, allowed their children to study religion from the outside looking in. My father, a former altar boy and my mother, a Methodist Sunday school teacher, patiently watched and waited as I searched through the muck that is the human perception of the afterlife.

Much of my interest in what I would call "the supernatural" grew during conversations with my Grandfather a French Canadian immigrant. Polimir Lawrence came from a zealous religious past that included everything from an extreme interest in the shadowy side of Catholicism to the family's history of faith healing. My sense of the past was tweaked as local and family history was instilled into me by my grandfather and father. I remember ghost stories that spoke of suicidal lighthouse keepers and long dead sheriffs having backed into the Manistique River. My Grandfather was a fantastic story teller that had easy opportunity to influence my young and curious mind.

My interest in the paranormal, although sometimes escaping me as it has been such a part of my life, is often apparent to others. In addressing a group about my history of paranormal study, I began my speech by re-living a 1992 midnight trip aboard the Queen Mary in California. Walking in the footsteps of Charlie Chaplin and Laurel and Hardy (whose full-size cardboard images at that time adorned the ship) excited and thrilled our lone squad of four. After the talk, my brother, Devin, reminded me that I had forgotten a few things, not limited to his first and only visit to a cemetery after dark in 1982. On further reflection,

3

Chapter 1

I was able to place my first paranormal investigation in the summer of 1974 at the age of twelve. Being fortunate enough to have a grandfather with a cassette tape recorder and being a student of Harry Houdini, I diligently marched my way up to the local cemetery to install my 60 minute tape system. This all in hopes of capturing what is now known as EVP or electronic voice phenomena. EVP is the disembodied voice or sound emitted by a spirit, and yes, I still have the tape.

I am sure I had all the same "ghost hunting" experiences that you and most others had as a child, but perhaps with a difference. When I was triple dog dared to touch the haunted house door, I always did. Incidents in my youth and teen years with local phenomena led me to Poe, King, Lovecraft, and a passionate urge to define the afterlife. College years found me pursuing a degree in Political Science and History, culminating in my history article: "*The Ghosts of Seney's Boot Hill*" in 1982. My study did not end there having subsequently visited hundreds of prominent sights including the Queen Mary, the Del Coronado, Greystone Asylum (before its demolition), the

Christian: Fayette EVP age 4

New Jersey Pine Barrens and even the mystical Voodoo huts of Haiti.

I brought my daughter Nicole into the fold toward the end of the 90's with local trips to Seul Choix Point, Fayette Ghost Town, multiple cemeteries, etc. My son Christian followed the family tradition in 2006 demonstrating a passion and talent for paranormal investigation that not only makes me proud, but often makes me chuckle. The UPST (Upper Peninsula Spook Team) was born with the first stories that my Grandfather imparted to me. Although I hunted for many years by myself or with the unwilling relative or girlfriend, investigating with an actual group is much more rewarding and thorough. I tied up with a relative who had discovered an interest in the paranormal and obviously wanted to scratch an itch. Although she is no longer with the team, her youngsters continue with the UPST to this day and all are academy certified. The team then added my athletic and committed nephew, the adrenalin-driven historian Bryson Lawrence.

"Brys" has become not only a respected investigator and instructor, but has led remote teams to other locations with  good old UPST knowhow. I love the picture of Brys in the morgue at a Northern Asylum. He is currently pursuing a degree at Grand Valley University, in *Millionaire 101,* while his Uncle has to man ongoing UPST Academies short handed, (Yes, I miss him).

Family friend Joseph LeDuc joined the team and also assists at academies. Although Joe's daytime job is working with animals, he maintains his paranormal pursuits and has been invaluable in checking out locations for future hunts.

Chapter 1

Family investigations have included several local destinations which I list here:

- Seul Choix Pointe lighthouse (a family favorite).
- Fayette Ghost Town.
- The Old D*********** estate (name hidden to protect descendents).
- The Jolly Inn (supposedly haunted by Captain Jolly and featured in a great book by author Jan Langley (*A Ghostly Road Tour of Michigan's Upper Peninsula*).
- The Famous House of Ludington.
- The Helmer House Inn.
- The Nahma Inn.
- The Mysterious Paulding Light.
- The Riverside, Old Cooks, Old Garden, Trudell, Fairview, Seney, Parkview, Manistique Lakeview cemeteries, and too many others to name here. Don't forget Day Hunts are effective training tools for the youngster too! You never know what may turn up in a photo.

The reason I listed a few of the many local sites the UPST has visited is to demonstrate that wherever you live, in as little as a half hour drive, you can get to an exciting ghost hunting destination. This will be covered in the chapter on the OZ (OrganiZation). Well, enough about us let's begin the hunt!

"AHHWOAHHHHH!"
I raced around the end of the building through the rain
with flashlight in hand.
My nephew Bryson knelt on one knee near a basement
window of the old building.

"What happened?" I asked breathlessly.

Bryson looked up at me with eyes like saucers,
*"I looked in the window with my flashlight, and a mannequin
kind of popped out at me."*

I realized how shocking this would have been
but I still had to laugh. On a ghost hunt, even when
nothing happens, something happens.

- Seul Choix Point Lighthouse 2009, 8:30 pm

2

In Search of?

Anomaly: Trans Allegheny Lunatic Asylum, W.VA.

Put simply, we are searching for evidence of life after death. Not everyone has an interest in this pursuit and some even have an outright fear. I have tried to enlist investigators for my team of intelligence, passion and depth but many times these same people have said no thanks. Whether a dread of the unknown or a possible challenge to their beliefs or sanity, some of the best candidates for paranormal investigation are unwilling to participate.

I have had the same questions myself. Will people think I'm crazy? Is calling on the spirits of the dead opening me up to the influence of evil? And lastly, is it contrary to my faith?

So that it's understood, I am a practicing Christian. In asking myself these questions, I have expanded my inquiry regarding the paranormal to others. This includes pastors, priests and even ordained ministers like those we now carry as members of our team. The answer is virtually always the same with sometimes additional qualifiers like:

> "Of course there are ghosts. The bible is riddled with them."

> "Jesus himself exorcised demons."

To sum it up, I have not spoken to a single religious authority that has ever asked me to stop my investigating due to faith. Only one has warned me about any element of the practice. A Catholic priest told me that if I ever encounter an entity that manifests as a man, it is only appearing in a human form so that we can relate and this is not a benevolent being. He went on to tell me that there are three different kinds of spirit manifestations that men primarily experience. The first is a vision of light or an angel that can help us or lead us to better things like: "Hail thee, behold the king of kings." The second is the type that assumes the guise of man, something that we're comfortable with, to entrap and fool us; malignant spirits. These two are among the primary entities encountered in paranormal investigation. He held the third type much more forbidding. It is called a demon or according to some religious beliefs, an elemental.

Yes, the UPST has been appealed to in many of these cases, but they are not the focus of this book or anything that you should be troubled about. Demonology is not an area that the ordinary paranormal squad usually investigates and you need not. In other words, if you receive an investigation request that appears to be of an unusual nature, handle it delicately. Call someone like the UPST or another experienced team and do not launch the hunt until the site has been checked out. We will tell you how to proceed. But keep in mind that 99.9% of paranormal investigation is intriguing, harmless family entertainment and has nothing to do with the above.

***

PART I Entities

So, let's tackle what kind of substantiation you are looking for when your team takes on a hunt. I will describe several types of entities and then further break them down into their different manifestations and forms of evidence. When looking for proof of life after death we endeavor to make contact with these entities. Here they are in five general categories:

- **Residual Spirit** – A residual is a spirit that goes through the same actions or activities on a repeating basis, usually inherent on the particular setting or situation of a life and location. Basically, this type of ghost has been imprinted upon the fabric of time. The theory behind the residual spirit ties closely to Electro Magnetic Field. Let's suppose that as assumed by most experienced paranormal investigators ghosts are tied to electric phenomena. Then it can be further supposed, as though on a magnetic recording tape, they  can leave an electronic impression on their physical surroundings to be replayed in perpetuity. It can also be surmised that living human beings who perform repetitive acts or have been part of an emotional or violent occurrence can leave an

11

imprint on this world to be repeated again and again. Manifestations, in this category of entity, can be anything from footsteps and sounds to an apparition. Keep in mind that although you won't get intelligent or responsive EVP from a residual spirit, it doesn't mean that this type of entity can't manifest itself into more than one of these five categories.

- **Intelligent Spirit** – The second category of spirit is labeled intelligent because it has the ability to interact with human beings. This is why we perform EVP sessions among other practices. An electronic voice phenomenon indicates an entity manifesting itself in an audio form that we can subsequently hear. But this is only one of several types of manifestations in which an intelligent spirit can make itself known. EMF to orbs to apparitions and kinetic movement are all possible and will be discussed in more detail at the end of the chapter. But for now, keep this in mind, an entity may be heard repeating the same steps he or she walked while alive, and what we perceive as that same spirit may independently manifest later for an EVP session with your team. It follows that this same ghost can also become angry and malevolent for any number of reasons. Thus, it is possible for a spirit to function independently of its residual appearance in an intelligent manner. Does this mean there are two different manifestations? Possibly, but just keep in mind that they don't have to be one or the other.

- **Malevolent Spirit** – A malevolent or malignant spirit is exactly what it implies, a mean spirit. This could be an entity that was bitter, violent, hurt or ill in their previous human form. These unbalanced spirits tend to act out in several ways. For instance, like asking that investigators simply leave or depart, scratching or oppressing one of the household family or team members. 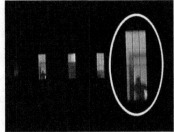 Oppression becomes apparent through feelings of dread, paranoia, nausea, etc. Scratching, along with oppression, is not uncommon conduct and although additionally occurring at some level in other categories, should never be accepted exclusively as a demonic entity. Sometimes demonic entities are classified as malevolent, but for our purposes in paranormal investigation we differentiate between the two. Still, when encountering a malevolent spirit extreme caution should be taken. Some teams opt to leave when asked to and provocation of spirits is something that the UPST advocates only in extreme cases. Provocation is the act of irritating or challenging a spirit in an effort to elicit a response. You will note some "paranormal investigators" are already provoking on the pre-hunt walk through. This is what happens when inexperienced individuals investigate or get their own television show. Don't employ this type of attention drawing gaffe when confronting a malevolent entity; exercise good common sense and respect for the dead.

- **Poltergeist** – Taken from the German term for "noisy ghost," the poltergeist is a rare entity demonstrative of kinetic activity and loud noise designed to frighten. Although they are extremely rare, it is theorized that poltergeists are more prevalent in homes where there is a prepubescent girl. Whether caused by a child or simply channeled through them is open to conjecture. But either way, poltergeists can also be representative of more than one category of entity and are not to be trifled with. Poltergeists may be more interactive than a malevolent spirit but the same rules of investigation apply. Call an experienced lineup to help you control the situation. House cleansings and even exorcisms have been used to remove these nasty houseguests. When encountering this type of entity rely on a knowledgeable team or authority until you feel comfortable.

- **Demonic Entity** – Also known as a demonic spirit or simply a demon (daemon). Most religions believe a demon is representative of evil or Satan. Whereas, these religions usually contrast demons with angels, other beliefs label them "elementals" with either good or evil bearing. Again, as I recommended earlier, these entities are not to be investigated without experience and absolute necessity. We have members of our team with over thirty years of paranormal investigation experience preferring not to take part. They are into the excitement of the ghost hunt and simply do not need the potential risk. My education in the area of demonology began at the age of seventeen for reason of my grandfather's theories and his passionate Catholicism. The study continued in the 1990's with my mission work in the country of Haiti and progressed with a young man from Milwaukee, Wisconsin who contacted me regarding a possession. Many cases have since transpired that have gained me contacts I call on if needed. These cases are not anything we look for but are something I feel obligated to continue. Some of this may be due to my experience diving for a search and rescue squad. As a scuba diver I worked with the

Luce West County Search and Rescue team and took part in a number of recoveries. It was not pleasant and I am grateful that  this pursuit didn't destroy my pleasure in the sport. This is how I view the UPST interaction with demonic entities; we are there to help, even though it will probably not be an enjoyable pursuit. It would take another book to fully address oppression, suppression and possession and you shouldn't address demonic entities at all. That is not without years of supervised experience in the field. Encountering demonic entities isn't like the movies and it is not a game. When addressing any case with extraordinary activity, always exercise informed caution. Remember that this sort of investigation is not part of a family oriented paranormal team and doesn't need to be part of yours. Just have fun.

***

Chapter 2
PART II Manifestations

The entities that we addressed in part one of this chapter can appear in a number of manners. Consider PART II as "what a spirit can do." I will now break these methods down into forms noticeable to an investigator, in other words, their basic manifestations.

- *Full Body Apparition* – The Mount Everest of paranormal investigation. Witnessing a full body apparition is comparable to the Detroit Lions winning the Super Bowl, although like Mt. Everest, full bodies have actually happened (sorry nephew Brys, I had to say it). A full body apparition is what it implies, a spirit from head to toe. It is the rarest of all manifestations and is almost never captured on film. Of the fifty or so UPST members nationwide with years of experience, only a few have witnessed such a treat.

- *Half Body Apparition* – Again in the description but includes most divisions of what otherwise would be a full body. Some believe half bodies are not able to gather the amount of energy necessary to fully manifest. Other times half bodies are seen partly obscured by objects, ground or walls that did not exist when their imprint was left on the locale.

- *Vocal Contact* – Sometimes an intelligent spirit attempts to communicate with us through verbal communication but in other instances a "voice" can simply be a residual event. This isn't difficult to differentiate: If you hear the voice responding to you it is an intelligent spirit. If the voice operates independently or on a regular schedule it is most likely residual. This is one of the more common yet fascinating ways that a spirit can demonstrate its presence and is usually discovered during the post investigation analysis.

On rare occasions a vocalization can be heard immediately with the naked ear or picked up with a spirit box or a real time recorder but as I pointed out, most are discovered after the hunt.

- *Touch* – A physical manifestation sometimes employed by an entity to make contact with an investigator. It is similar to vocal contact in that it can also be requested by an investigator that is not faint of heart. Unlike most vocalizations by a spirit, touch will be experienced immediately and can often be a bit startling. Residual spirits are the only category of entity that cannot knowingly employ touch although cold spots may be your accidently making contact with a residual. Malevolent scratching is not enjoyable but provable. Unfortunately, most occurrences usually fall under the heading of "personal experience" as it is difficult to substantiate with other than an infrared thermometer. This practice will be explained in the chapter on equipment.

- *Sound Abnormalities* – You have heard the expression, "things that go bump in the night?" Yes they do, and with the proper recording devices these bumps go from manifestation to evidence very neatly. In a later case study at Seul Choix Pointe Lighthouse, I describe how something dropping on an upstairs floor in all likelihood was paranormal activity. One of the most popular tools of every paranormal investigator is the old "shave and a haircut" ploy. All that's involved is to tap out the "shave and a haircut" tune and wait for the "two bits" conclusion from our ghostly pals in response. Another use for the manifestation of sound abnormality is to ask an entity to respond with a knock or even more specifically, one knock for yes and two for no. You will be surprised at how often you get results.

- *Shadows or Black Masses* – Shadows are often seen on investigations. Sometimes in corners and often out of the corner of the eye. They can also be indicative of an energy drain in a particular location which is also coupled with ghostly manifestations. A black mass may be one of the scarier ways an entity can manifest and is often associated with cold spots. Although sometimes akin to the shadow, it often has the ability to move, block light and even appear human (shadow people). It is also sometimes associated with non-human shapes (evil). Again a drain on or the lack of viable energy may be the reason black masses don't appear fully materialized. Or perhaps this type of apparition is an intelligent or malevolent entity favoring this dark manifestation.

- *Mists* – Ectoplasm is a luminous substance, believed  gel-like or sometimes a mist. It is thought to emanate when an entity pierces dimensions upon its manifestation.

  Sometimes it is just a mist and at other times can surround an apparition.

Often this ectoplasmic discharge is apparent to the naked eye. It can also be photographed and videotaped with the proper lighting. Most paranormal investigators believe that mists and other visual manifestations utilize ectoplasm to become visible and on occasion an entity can leave behind an actual gel like residue. Although we carry a collection kit containing rubber gloves, swatches, and Petri dishes, in hundreds of investigations it has seldom left our storage trunk. Don't let this discourage you, be prepared and if you get slimed, you may be the team that tips the world of paranormal investigation on its ear.

- *Cold Spots* – A common occurrence in all categories of entity manifestation. We have discussed how the use of energy by a spirit attempting contact can lead to a fall in temperature in the same locale but I should also mention that in rare cases, upward swings in temperature can also be indicative of spirit manifestation. As I said earlier, there are ways to verify these temperature variations that will be covered later in the book.

- *Oppression* – It is believed that some malevolent entities have the ability to induce a sense of foreboding, dizziness, nausea, paranoia or outright fear. Some spirits take pleasure in upsetting the applecart of normal human activity for a variety of reasons. They range from accidental to the mischievous. As you will discover in subsequent chapters this is a common occurrence and the UPST has even experienced the loss of members through some of our hunts due to what may have been oppression. If someone on your team experiences any of the symptoms above, have them leave the building or location. After they are out of range examine the site for what may be other more conventional causes of their affliction. I will mention a few here: Methane is a gas common to old buildings due to the build up of bat guano in the walls and attics. Excessive methane can cause nausea and illness. Also be aware that other flammable gases like natural gas and propane and even septic drain gas can cause the same symptoms. It never hurts to have a plumber or a heating and cooling man on your team. The UPST also carries a gas detector that has come in handy in these particular applications. Oppression can also be caused by what is known as a fear cage. A fear cage is commonly found in locations where the wiring is not grounded such as older houses or hospitals. The electricity that runs throughout these aged facilities actually surrounds us with an electro magnetic field. This is easily picked up with an EMF detector and should be taken into account when defining the activity monitored during the hunt. When there is a high level of electrical current in an area, the fear cage created has the tendency to intensify ordinary experiences and activity into what can be perceived as colossal events. In other words, the sound of a popgun can transform into that of a shotgun. The last alternate clone of oppression is directly attached to the investigator. Make sure that everyone is in good spirits and health before an investigation is begun. An illness seldom improves in a cold building in the wee hours of the morning.

- *Orb* – Literally a sphere or ball of light. Many believe that orbs can indicate the partial manifestation of any category of spirit. Orbs are often caught in digital photographs and occasionally on video but in almost all instances they can be explained by insects or dust. Be especially wary of dust because, contrary to popular belief, it doesn't always fall downward but can be caught like a tempest in a whirlwind. Occasionally, there is a

Photo 1: Tyical Orb   Photo 2: Paulding Sprite (Orb?)

location where a connection between the activity being experienced and the orbs being captured merit more consideration. Although the UPST doesn't give much credence to orbs in digital photographs, we have logged many worthy of a second look. The Paulding Light is one of those rare and special places where excess electrical energy almost always produces an orb or two. At the Paulding Light, members of our team have not only captured orbs of different color, but on one summer excursion, we caught what appears to be a sprite on two different digital cameras. I initially believed it to be an insect of some sort until later when I received a website from Lisa Miller who had taken one of the photographs. The webpage was out of the British Isles and had multitudes of "fairy" and "sprite" images from all over the world mirroring Lisa's photo. I am still skeptical but as I say in my academy instruction, at the very least orbs are fun. Take loads of photographs; you never know what you may catch.

***

PART III Evidence

Here, I will describe what evidence we hope to obtain in proving a spirit's manifestation. View it as "what my tools and I can detect."

- EVP - Electronic voice phenomena or EVP is the disembodied voice or sound emitted by a spirit spontaneously or when questioned. This type of evidence is procured through recording and receives a classification. For instance, an intelligent, intelligible response to a question is a Class A EVP. Some

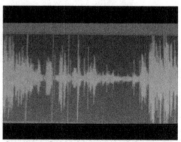
Computer software deconstruct of Fayete EVP

investigators have made Class A anything understandable; the UPST has set higher standards. Class B EVP contains a clearly audible and understandable sound but may or may not be intelligible. Most EVP evidence falls into Class C due to poor quality and high levels of white noise (hiss in all frequencies).

- Photographic Evidence – I just described orb manifestations and how they can be documented. Photographic evidence has also been used to record every form of manifestation except oppression, touch and vocal contact. In addition, thanks to thermal imagers, you may even get a picture of a cold or hot spot.

- Video Evidence – This is the rarest type of evidence and the most astonishing if captured. The UPST keeps a reserve of infrared cameras and we usually have several running from the beginning of the hunt until the end. I will talk about this later in the

equipment section of the book but remember the video camera is not only a source of video; it can also be an excellent source of audio. In addition, it is also a lot more fun to do the post hunt analysis as a face or two caught unaware is always good for a snicker.

- <u>Sensory Evidence</u> – In most cases this type of evidence falls into the class of personal experience. A cold spot or draft, a strange odor or even a touch are all personal experiences that with few exceptions cannot be verified by our equipment. The UPST has conducted investigations rich with personal experience of sensory evidence and have not been able to nail down anything conclusive with our equipment. Conversely, we have had monotonous investigations that later revealed a stockpile of EVP and sound anomalies in the post analysis. Be attuned to your senses when investigating and keep your tools ready, you may just have company.

- <u>EMF</u> – It is theorized that an electro magnetic field is altered by a spirit when manifesting. Always get initial baseline readings so that you know what ambient EMF is present. This will make later abnormal levels obvious. You will find that some cell sensors have more than one sensitivity setting. The proper setting will become apparent on your baseline reading walk through.

- <u>Kinetic Interaction</u> –The dictionary definition is: produced by motion. In the paranormal field, kinetic means movement and in fact we look for this motion to be produced by different entities. This can be spontaneous or requested movement, as when the UPST sets our ghost traps, but in both cases we have measureable or filmable evidence. We have run into everything from objects flying off of tables to marbles rolling at our request. More on this later in the book.

- <u>Temperature Variables</u> – Rapid changes in ambient or surface temperatures can be evidence of a presence. We have discussed how entities draw on energy making it colder but occasionally they will cause something to heat up. I will go into what tools to use and how to discern this type of evidence in the chapter on equipment.

"WHAT THE CRAP WAS THAT?"
Robert looked at Christian and me.

It was a wet and rainy July day and the UPST had already finished the first half of our hardcore outside hunt weekend at the Paulding Light the night before. We had been scoping out woodland trails before dark near our campground at Cedar River for that evening's Sasquatch hunt. This spot had been host to two Bigfoot sightings in the last eighteen months.

"I don't know?"
I smiled referring to the low and eerie howl we'd just heard.
"Sounded like a Bigfoot," Christian remarked.
"Yes it did," I chuckled having been informed earlier
what was going on.

Linda Caron met us as we returned to our campsite.
"Did you hear that?" Robert asked her.
"Oh, that was just Jaime…" she said referring to her son, one of our
newer members.

It turns out that our actor in company, Jaime, had a bullhorn and an amazing Bigfoot impression. We made plans to later spoof the other campers with the howl of the elusive Sasquatch.

- J.W. Wells Campground - Cedar River, Michigan, 6:54 pm

26

3

The Kid Factor

The inclusion of my children in my historical and paranormal investigation has drawn the praise of most but occasionally the ire of others. In all honesty, I have found that most condemnation comes from those who do not have the motivation or the knowledge to share the life lessons that history can offer. For instance, if you are separated or divorced, be very careful about surprising the other parent with a statement like: "We're staying overnight in a haunted house this weekend." It should be understood that ignorance is the best weapon of a lazy parent. Anyone doing something outside the norm can and will be called out on any activity remotely approaching creative parenting time. This includes everything from sports to snorkeling to ghost hunts.

Chapter 3

If difficulties with your spouse or ex-mate transcend simple jealousy or stupidity, I suggest you consult a professional behavioral health specialist for an endorsement. In recent years, cemetery and genetic study have become an activity of focused interest kept alive by only a few, whereas a mere forty years ago children learned their family history in a graveyard. Sometimes the old ways are the best ways and in believing just that, I have discussed my theories on paranormal investigation and cemetery history with many psychologists who endorse the time sharing and educational opportunities offered by these activities. It is a fun and exciting way to learn.

When speaking with a naysayer, don't be swayed by what at first may appear to be viable argument, but opt for  logic and tried and true practice. What I am saying can best be summed up in a disagreement I had with a relative many years ago. One of my daughter's favorite movies was *Chitty Chitty Bang Bang*. Remember the one with Dick Van Dyke? My relative felt that her children should not watch this movie due to a particularly scary scene in the middle featuring a character called the *Child Catcher*. Understandably, she was concerned that her children would be impacted by this terrifying scene. Now on first glance, this seems to make total sense, after all these were her children. I asked just one question:

"So you think it's a bad thing that your children are afraid of a stranger trying to lure them into a vehicle with candy?"

My point is simple. Sometimes the first take on an activity or lack thereof is not the correct one, and oftentimes people don't take the time to study an activity before making a decision about it, looking instead to find something wrong. Interestingly, this is the story of my first child's entrance into cemetery field trips. I was actually criticized for including my daughter in the upkeep of her great-grandparent's graves on Memorial Day. Separation between people often closes options and turns off minds. The pertinent and wonderful thing about paranormal research is that those involved must maintain an open mind; it is a necessity.

When we talk about children and paranormal investigation, the first thing that we should understand is the child's role in the paranormal. One aspect of paranormal research studies the ability of the human psyche to transmit and

Parnormal Investigation is fun for kids of all ages! (and Herby!)

receive information through other than normal senses: touch, smell, taste, sight and hearing. We have all seen *The Sixth Sense*, which had to do with a sensitive child. What the young psychic boy practiced is what's now called "psychic" or "empathic," although we have in the past called it ESP, or extra sensory perception. This encompasses many facets, including an attunement to paranormal activity. For terms of our discussion we will break down

29

Chapter 3

ESP into two main categories: telepathy and clairvoyance. Telepathy is the ability to communicate without speech, other discourse or physical interaction. Yep: "reading minds." A clairvoyant is able to draw a picture or narrative from interaction with places, events or even physical objects. Neither telepathy nor clairvoyance are limited to our time continuum but can function within the past or the realm of what is yet to be. Seeing the future in dreams or through "psychic ability" as well as being attuned to a paranormal knowledge of the past are both common manifestations. Skeptics will doubt while those of us that are open to the phenomena of ESP watch as more and more police investigations employ psychic profilers and mediums for leads in criminal homicide cases.

One well-recognized norm of psychics is that they seem to show ability at a young age. Again, depending upon the parents, the culture, and the religion, these children can be seen as strange, disturbed or in the worst cases, possessed. Usually, these talented young people are encouraged by their parents to dismiss their visions as dreams or simply to stand mute. Some youngsters even hide their ability or suppress it in an effort to be "normal." Even as an adult, I am sure that you have learned to guard your interest in the paranormal as I have, insulating yourself from those that choose to attack and ridicule what they don't understand.

And now, we must address the question that we have been dancing around: "Are children actually more sensitive to the paranormal?" My quick answer: yes, or, most of them are. My son was brought into the fold not only through family practice, but due to an incident at the rental house of his mother. It seems that he was seeing a lady in a white dress at his mother's rental. He would stoically describe her as: *"A mother with no children."*

It turns out that the wife of the landlord had been killed in an auto accident years earlier and he and his daughters had actually had incidents so extreme that they had called in a local pastor to perform a cleansing. The erratic emotional behavior of my son's mother as well as his fear of sleeping in his own bed convinced me that I had best teach him to classify experiences such as these into a realm of fun, science and parental acceptance. Enter paranormal investigation.

A good parent or teacher does not ignore or deny the existence of a child's nature but instead works to nurture it (unless your kid's last name is Dahmer). Those who berate a spiritual world while using a child as a simple tool are the same parents that will lock the child in a closet for "their own protection."

My mother, a very spiritual person, had an interesting theory on children and the paranormal. She told me this about my son:

"David, all babies have a memory of heaven. Some lose it quickly, and some hold it. You can see it in their

eyes. Christian still remembers heaven." Initially I took this comment as a very nice thing that my mother had said about my boy. But as time went on I began to recall and realize how in tune my mother was with what most would call the "supernatural" or "paranormal" and how correct she was in her appraisal of my son's connection to the spiritual. I fondly recall in around 1999 my Mother's effort with my family team of father Rudy, sister Shannon, aunt Joyce and myself to be the next family on *Scariest Places on Earth.* We didn't make the cut, but my Mom was classic!

A child's tale of the paranormal, if digested without bias, usually has more credibility than that of an adult. As I illustrated earlier through my own son's experience, a young mind gives credence to the description of a paranormal encounter. He had no previous knowledge or history of the house. He was not old enough to have developed the social wherewithal to make up such an experience. This innocence combined with an inability to distinguish between the normal and the paranormal or even Mickey Mouse and a real mouse makes his sighting much more credible. Ironically the inability to distinguish between what is and isn't real seems to aid a child in his or her overall sensitivity to paranormal phenomena. This inert knowledge is a gift that we, as adults, abandoned long ago.

So, having children along on a paranormal investigation can only create an additional capacity to understand the spiritual realm - a boon to any paranormal team and a catharsis for the sensitive child. Sensitivity is the foundation of experience within the young. Children have not developed the skepticism and prejudice that we as adults have come to embrace. I believe that, in imposing these filters, God has triggered in adults a tool to simplify and streamline our lives, whereas the lack of these filters obviously leaves the young heart and mind in a more open state. Some believe that the young brain or mind is just simply more receptive to stimulus and paranormal phenomena such as near death experiences, past life remembrances, psychic ability and spirit interaction. Whatever it is, it is effortless to argue the fact that children are more attuned to all that is life, including that which is not documented, classified or understood.

So, when is a child mature enough to participate in an organized ghost hunt? I impose a few easy to understand standards or "acid tests," if you will. I have organized these assessments under the acronym PASS.

To put it succinctly, after employing the following assessments, you should know full well whether you and your child have *passed* the steps pertinent to beginning this exciting hobby or whether you will wait another year and attempt to PASS them again.

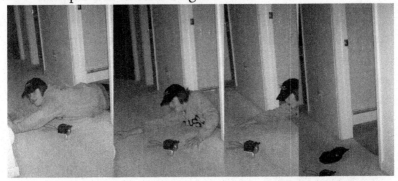

Remember: Kids are kids and Ghost Hunts are fun!

The first of these is without a doubt the most important of the elements and in fact is from where all other requirements on the scale develop. The P is for Parental Evaluation. This point transcends the simple evaluation of your child to the more complex self-introspection necessary in taking any step forward in family paranormal investigation. In looking at your child, you must primarily look at their overall developmental level. One test that I use is what I call the "Kindergarten List."

Chapter 3

Your little ghost hunter should be capable of following at least three directives in a row and in order. The above evaluation template places the starting age at approximately six to eight for most children and as young as five for the special few.

In applying the second analysis to measure your child's immediate suitability for ghost hunting, you must ask yourself does he (or she) have any "interest?" If they enjoy *R.L. Stine* and *Scooby Doo*, this is a plus. If they like to watch ghost hunting shows and the *History Channel*, their interest is a given. If not, don't be concerned as there are many developmental activities that can be planned with your child to nurture an interest in history and the unexplained. These will be covered later in this chapter.

The second part of Parental Evaluation is every bit important as the first. Self-introspection often times makes it more difficult to maintain any objectivity. When

addressing your own capacity as a parent and potential hunt leader, ask yourself the following:

- Do you have the knowledge and or facilities to organize and research a ghost hunt for your family?

- Do you have the patience necessary to work on an intimate level with children?

- And last but not least, do you have a passion for history and the mysterious?

If you answered no to any of the above, paranormal investigation may not be for you and your family.

The second item on the PASS scale is "a" for the *Aesop's Fables* appraisal. This is an observation which takes into account your child's simple ability to accept and understand outcome. A sense of "outcome" may seem a little heavy, but let me embellish. We all recall Hansel and Gretel, but do you remember that both of the children having misbehaved were threatened with being cooked by the witch or in the end, her own horrible fate? Fables usually have a moral message and sometimes do not end happily, but they do build a concept of existence and outcome. If you have ever read a story like this to your child and found that it abnormally disturbed them, the gravestone of a youth that died in 1918 from the influenza epidemic may be difficult to explain. Does this mean that everyone who participates in paranormal investigation should have a complete understanding of life, death and the great beyond? Not at all; who does? What it means is that your child should have some perception of being. The complications and intricacies of life are often more easily viewed through the buoyant nature of a parable or fable. Again, acceptance of "outcome" makes a world of the paranormal and a plausible "afterlife" easier first to acknowledge and then to enjoy.

Needless to say, the intangible benefits of fables or stories also give a sense of narrative and resultant history which transfer beneficially to the investigation experience. Evaluating whether your child is ready to PASS into family ghost hunting is as easy as listening to their thoughts post-fable. Reading stories to your child is always good, but now you can read to your child with increased purpose!

Chapter 3

The first "s" of our PASS is named not only from my youth but also from how I personally taught my children the art of "silence." The Sunday Go to Meetin' assessment is basically silence emboldened. This PASS acid test is very basic and easy to employ. Go to church or any public function that requires good manners. If your child is not capable of behaving or sitting through a Sunday service, and you as a parent are not capable of controlling them, the possibility of a monotonous investigation is also something that neither of you would adapt to successfully.

If your child mutters any of the following:

"I'm hungry"

"I have to go to the bathroom"

"When are we going?"

"How long have we been here?"

These statements all equate to "I'm bored," and your child is probably not ready to PASS the Sunday go to Meetin' Silence test quite yet. The nice thing about this step on the PASS scale is that you get to keep on trying and no matter what the result, you will become a better disciplinarian; moreover your children will continue to reap the benefits of the resulting good behavior that you have instilled in them for the rest of their lives.

The last measure on the scale may be the most easily understood. I call it the Splash Mountain Recall. The benefits of this calculation are immediately obvious. Of course, there are exceptions, but if your child is old enough to ride on Splash Mountain, Space Mountain or any other frightening ride with no ill effect, fearful memories or nightmares, then they are usually old enough to family ghost hunt. If they ask to go on the ride again you are well on your way. Again the tests above are but rules of thumb that you as a parent should feel free to tweak in deference to your own child's demeanor, interest, and maturity.

To make this clear I now summarize the PASS points:

- **P**arental Evaluation (measures parental aptitude, child interest and maturity).

- **A**esop's Fable Test (provides a tool through which to observe your child's awareness in understanding and accepting outcome and existence).

- **S**unday Go to Meetin' Silence Test (easily establishes the emotional maturity of the child in different situations and locales).

- **S**plash Mountain Test (asks if your child is ready to enjoy unsettling excitement with no ill after-affects).

Lastly, if in applying my PASS system, you have determined that your child or you are not quite ready for the challenge of paranormal investigation, I promised to help. First, develop a new leisure activity schedule with your child that includes a beginning approach to research. If once or twice a week you can turn on The History Channel or another educational source, you will find oodles of interesting programming which you can enjoy with your child and then go to the internet and double up on the research. What I mean is that no matter how well a documentary is produced, there is always more to the story that has been left unsaid. A good book or an old TCM movie can, of course, produce the same passion for the "real" or "unknown" storyline. The internet gives us the option to pursue this information almost immediately. By reading the biographies of historical figures and old movie stars on sites such as Wikipedia.org and IMDB.com your child will discover the deeper understanding that these "inanimate objects" supplying our entertainment were once real people. This empathetic awareness of humanity and history readily transfers to paranormal investigation.

Secondly, pick out a good ghost hunting show to watch once a week. I admit, there aren't many "good" ones, but give it a try. I shouldn't recommend any particular show as I may be biased having friends in the field, but I can tell you this: stay away from shows that include physics, empaths, or clairvoyants. I will go into detail on this in our next chapter "Forming the Team."

My last surefire method for introducing your mini investigator to the fun and excitement of history and the paranormal is as simple as two words: "Day Hunt."

Both of my children began the trek to ghost hunting curiosity in the same way. Visiting historical landmarks, national parks, restaurants, etc., that have an interesting history and sometimes even involving the paranormal. As a parent, research is a must so that you can escape the organized tour opting for a one-on-one instruction session with your child instead. My son was executing his own EVP recordings at such places as Fayette Ghost Town before he was even in kindergarten. His respect for and understanding of history was nurtured at a very early age. Day hunts provide the teaching parent an opportunity to introduce the child to the excitement of a hunt in a less intense setting and thereby slowly building the interest and the urge to take part in future full-fledged night investigations.

So does this mean that we should make midget ghost hunters out of every child over forty-eight inches tall who can sit quietly while following orders? Quick Answer: NO! This is primarily a parental decision which must be based on two important factors: First, is the child ready? And more importantly, are the parents ready to step up and accomplish the research necessary to organizing a quality investigation? If these answers are yes, then off you go!

"Oh shoot," I grunted as I leaned over the infrared camera and tripod next to the bed. "I forgot the EMF. It must be downstairs…I'll be right back."

My son Christian, already tucked in, nodded his head in accord. I walked down the shadowed stairwell in search of the EMF detector. The second half of our squad, my nephew Bryson, and family friend Joe Leduc had just left for home, and it seemed they had hidden the tool. After several minutes, I found it under a bag of Dill Pickle Potato Chips and headed back upstairs. I stopped dead in my tracks.

There was a voice coming from an upstairs bedroom.

I quickly realized it was my son.

"Thank you for letting us stay here, Captain Townshend," Christian spoke aloud. "The bed is very comfortable…"

I smiled as I entered the room.

"I'm proud of you my son," I laughed. "You didn't miss me at all."

Christian not knowing I was standing in the doorway looked up abruptly and smiled.

"I was just talking with Captain Townshend."

As he continued, his face showed an insight far beyond his years.

"I feel very comfortable here… I feel at home."

- Seul Choix Point Lighthouse, January 31, 2009, 2:30 am

4

Forming the Team

So here you are. You have the inclination, you have the family and they have all stepped up to PASS into the ranks of future paranormal investigators. The question is "how do I start the team?"

First of all, let me be clear on something before beginning the instruction on team formation. We have all heard the much used phrase, "there is no *I* in team." In the area of paranormal investigation, this phrase brings only one thought to my mind: "BULL PUCKEY!"

Although the "no *I* in team" slogan may come back in future team work discussion, for now focus on the "I." There is no team yet and if you want to form a working squad, consider this organization a communist dictatorship like the one under Emperor Obama. No one is going to give you support in starting a team until <u>you</u> initiate ground rules; organize the team and the investigation. By necessity you are the Lead Investigator.

Chapter 4

So where do you start? The answer is easy: with you and your child or with another interested relative. That means if you are a kid, you must convince your father or mother, grandparent, uncle, brother, sister or cousin to participate in your new hobby. The first thing you need is a teammate. There is plenty of time to categorize the team roles later on and after you have a recruit, you'll have a reason and a purpose to organize.

So now you have achieved the first prerequisite and you have a partner in crime; a confidante and a collaborator to bounce ideas off of and to help carry the work load. In screening this second member, make sure that they have a passion and interest that rivals your own. For instance, if you choose your cousin, make sure that he has a similar vision of paranormal investigation after you introduce your idea to form a team. This will be demonstrated in his immediately coming up with at least ten ideas, nine of which you disagree with but listen to and acknowledge anyway. If you are a parent starting a family team, concentrate on the PASS scale outlined in the previous chapter for all members and you are halfway there. Another important consideration in initial team make-up is whether you are an adult or a child; make sure your third member is an adult. If you are a kid, having an adult on board opens up several new horizons including driving, supervision and late night hunts. I know this as I have served as the wacky uncle director for many family adventures over the years. As a parent, the second adult becomes a partner with whom to share organization, planning, car pooling, etc., and without going into detail, it is always good to have extra supervision built into a team that travels with children. Let me suffice it to say that Sunday family dinner at grandma's will be very lively indeed if several members are discussing the last hunt and planning the next. Watch your little band grow.

Roles within a paranormal team are not an initial necessity but after your core members are on board these designations will become extremely helpful. You will find as the leader and person that started the team that you will own all titles in the beginning. This tact will aid you in getting the ball rolling but is not beneficial in the long term.

Let's talk about the many roles in your typical paranormal group. We have already covered some of the attributes that you as the "leader" or Lead Investigator should possess. Some of the qualities that must be inherent are passion, organizational skills, access to family and potential team members, as well as the totalitarian vision to take charge in the short term. Taking on the role of team leader is not all autographs and radio interviews. It is a no thanks job that requires your finding locales, making initial contact with the owners of said premises, naming the team, time, etc. We will have an additional breakdown of the basic roles and team duties at the end of the chapter, but hang on for now as I quickly run through them.

In an emergent team, another important position to designate is that of Researcher. This team member will make it their priority to help the team leader find haunted locales and will explore and document additional history for the next investigation. As time progresses, the researcher may take over all scheduling and initial research for the team presenting this information to the team leader for organization of the hunt.

The team Technical or Equipment Manager is exactly what the title implies. This person should have a working knowledge of all of your team's ghost hunting paraphernalia, as well as being responsible for dispersing equipment based on the team leader's assignments. Additionally, when the hunt is over, the tech manager is accountable for checking the equipment back into the storage locker. In addressing a team member's aptitude for the role of Tech Manager, ask him if he can set the clock on a DVD player or can download an I-Pod. Although I state this with tongue firmly planted in cheek, this type of electronic adeptness is truly a measure that can be indicative of tech management suitability.

In the age of the internet, every team should have a Computer Technician (Geek). Before the investigation the geek will upload related information in conjunction with the team leader and or researcher for the rest of the team to examine. This includes but is not limited to Video Pre-hunts, Hunt Location history and Cemetery directory internet sites. For example, although the administrators of *Findagrave* may be short sighted, inaccurate and arrogant, the website can occasionally be helpful if a cemetery is on the agenda. The computer tech or geek is also the person responsible for the downloading of post-hunt information (audio, video and photos) as well as teaming up with the tech manager and perhaps an investigator to analyze any evidence. Your geek will also be in charge of your internet website. This site should not only provide your team access to the above info, but should allow file sharing privileges and information on upcoming or potential locations. We will address these online specifics in a following chapter that addresses the internet and team possibilities.

Lastly, the heart of the team and the ghost hunting grunt so to speak: the Investigator. The following description encompasses three different levels of investigator. The first type is the IIT or the Investigator in Training. Other affectionate terms for the IIT are newbie, rookie or fish. The IITs primary function is to learn. Investigation is secondary to the learning process but in most cases these two duties run hand in hand. IITs always look forward to becoming a full fledged investigator and I recommend that your Lead Investigator mark the occasion with some special trial activity; perhaps a solo lock down…☺

The second level is full fledged Investigator. This designation involves not only basic investigative duties but often times becoming an assistant tech manager, researcher and evidence analyst. In addition, the Investigator will often be paired in an investigation with an IIT (newbie) for purposes of training and observation. An Investigator will have as many duties as they can responsibly handle and in time will become your future Tech Managers, Researchers and Leads.

The third type is the Lead, Leader or Lead Investigator which we have already discussed.

This is a good opportunity to summarize the five primary designations of a paranormal team and their basic duties:

- LEAD INVESTIGATOR – Also known as the Leader or Lead is responsible for selecting the team, organizing the hunt, contacting the proper owners or authorities and  dispersing the resulting evidence. My son felt

45

that this photo was the proper personage of the team leader. I am not a fan of Hitler, but I realize that at times the team leader must lead.

- RESEARCHER – Presents potential investigations to the Lead and then provides the  direction, history and myths of the chosen paranormal location. Works with the Geek to post pre-hunt information for team members to access. May also become an Investigator and Analyst if required.

- TECH MANAGER – Also known as "Q" maintains a working knowledge of the team's equipment, while continually searching for new cutting edge tools and techniques to aid the team in their explorations. This person will also confer with the Leader regarding equipment allocation amongst the team, and then subsequently handling dispersal and collection. Since the Q should be well versed in the function and potential anomalies of all the equipment, he is usually one of the primary post-hunt analysts.

- COMPUTER TECHNICIAN – Also referred to as Computer Expert, Computer Geek or just plain Geek. The Geek is primarily responsible for the conveyance of post-hunt media through the group website. In addition to website maintenance, the Geek also often becomes an evidentiary analyst. Sometimes aiding the researcher in delivering post-hunt information to the team. He is almost always impossible to find, but after missing for up to two weeks, can accomplish what he has put off in as little as just fifteen minutes.

- INVESTIGATOR – Responsible for the hands on work of an investigation and functioning on three levels.
  - Investigator in Training - aka IIT, newbie, rookie, fish.
  - Investigator – Full fledged ghost hunter.
  - Lead Investigator – the Leader or Lead person on the team or squad.

***

After you have established your primary team, there are a couple of other types of hunters you should be prepared to encounter: Guest Investigators and Psychic/Mediums. I will touch on these briefly.

Guest Investigators should not be a member's mother, father, brother or recommendation unless they are experienced investigators having a special skill set to offer the team. Some standards have to be set for inclusion on a hunt; team size and pre-hunt training being two. Of course, the numbers optimal for the location, seniority and first call-first serve are all ways of managing the team roster. In addition, our team has a training class we call the UPST

Chapter 4

Academy. This is a two hour session that walks prospective members through much of what you are now reading, along with hands on use of equipment followed by a supervised hunt. We do charge a nominal fee for the class after which the cadet is graduated to an Investigator in Training. The reason there is a fee is two fold. First, it helps to allay team overhead like website domain costs and subscriptions to such tools as Ancestry.com. Secondly, it separates the wheat from the chaff. Everybody would take a class if it was free but only passionate adventurers will make an investment. These are the very people that will be reliable teammates. In a nutshell, after you have established your team, be discerning in selecting or accepting guest investigators.

As for Psychics/Mediums/Clairvoyants/Empaths or whatever they choose to call themselves these days, I have had few legitimate interactions. For instance, in conducting the UPST Academies, I have seldom met a female cadet who hasn't told me that she is at least a "sensitive." Don't misunderstand me, there may be "female intuition," but it is principally based on unspoken communication such as body language and facial expressions or mannerisms. The ability to pick up on any afore mentioned elements aid in assessing almost all situations involving other human beings. But this doesn't make one a psychic or an empath. In fact, some of the empaths that I have worked with were more sociopath than psychic. The UPST makes it a rule to avoid investigating with a self-proclaimed psychic the first time at any location. There are two ways to look at it. If the person mistakenly believes they have extra-sensory perception, they may be unreserved with their opinion and muddy the scientific waters. If they are actually sensitive, they may be unreserved with their opinion and muddy the scientific waters. If you do chose to hunt with a psychic, be sure it is at location where you have already established scientifically documented baseline activity. Make sure that the psychic is accompanied as many prefer to carry no equipment and to wander. This is not an intelligent or effective practice in gathering evidence, so provide constant backup. Also, ask that they remain quiet until directed to open themselves up and then guard what the whole team hears. Going into an investigation with knowledge of the particular location activity is fine but being directed to supposed activity can happen; especially when the director is an inept sensitive. The unseasoned investigator is likely to be swayed by statements like:

"I feel a man in this room."

"There is something in the attic."

Keep an open mind when it comes to psychics but also keep an open mind that many times they are wrong, delusional or faking it. Genuine psychics are few and far between, so be open and appreciative if you find one, but practice the scientific method and be a skeptic and debunker first.

***

In ending this chapter on team formation, there are a few final thoughts I would like you to keep in mind. Although ghost hunting is a rapidly growing hobby, it is still an activity practiced by few. You are special and should remember that this pursuit, although becoming more popular, is not as main-stream as playing Scrabble or Play Station. Do not announce your recruitment at a party for instance. You will either be viewed as a nut or end up with twenty volunteers and only a few showing up, never to return. Bear in mind that not everyone will have the time, interest or commitment necessary to being part of a paranormal team. These individuals will show a great enthusiasm at first but after one or two investigations will become inaccessible and unavailable. Everyone has a paranormal itch to scratch and after one or two experiences,

some need never scratch it again. If this happens with any team member, no matter how promising, let it go. After the initial recruitment is made, give them one or two hunt notifications and then let them come to the team. Expect this type of person to believe they are doing the team a favor by simply showing up. It is never worth the time and effort to convince someone to have fun. If they don't get it, they don't get it.

The team should be formed one member (or two if they are related) at a time and on an intimate basis. This better allows you to observe the level of enthusiasm one on one. If a potential team member approaches you, remember that almost everyone will try ghost hunting once. Always look for a past long term commitment in the history of the potential candidate, as this indicates the passion necessary to count on future commitment. By this, I mean: a college degree, a child in school, a job, etc.

Invariably, you will have another member parent or child ask if someone they know can accompany your team on a hunt. Tell them to have the potential hunter call you personally as this shows some of the initiative necessary to demonstrate more than passing interest. If the candidate is a child, discuss it with his or her parents and make sure that they understand what is involved before giving their approval. You don't want to be dropping a fifteen year old off at 3:00 am in the morning with the local sheriff waiting at his home. Additionally, always identify the parent who thinks their child is the most mature tool in the shed. Any over exuberant parental brag is usually indicative of the opposite and is easily exposed by simply asking the parent to perform PASS and to present you with the results. I give you permission to blame it on this book. If the parent is insulted or unwilling to perform this essential task, rest assured that they would be poor future team members. This is the same person who will behave as though they are doing you and your squad a favor. Without knowing, they have already demonstrated a self aggrandizing posture that undermines the concept of "team." Never sacrifice your investigation and more importantly, the integrity of your team to be the nice guy. You may also run into a parent whose child is ready to hunt but the parent is overprotective. This type of pampering behavior should be an immediate disqualifier for your team. I recall when I was directing a fifth grade children's camp a few years ago and was approached by a young lady interested in becoming a counselor. Asking around about the sixteen year old I discovered that she came highly recommended as having great grades and outstanding maturity. When I called her father to sign a permission slip I was confronted with this:

"She's just a kid, who's going to watch her? Is there swimming? Are there boys?"

I politely answered all of this parent's questions concluding that he trusted few people, including his daughter. It was clear that if I put this girl on staff, I would have to care for both she and her father. This leads to the question: Who cares for the cabin of ten year olds? The moral of the story is this: Wait until the volunteer or future member returns and doesn't need parental permission. Hoping for this type of parent to grow up is fruitless. Let it go and you will save yours team undue disruption.

Keep your team intimate. What I mean by this is that you should know your team and their personalities. Never take more Newbies (Investigators in Training) than you have experienced personnel to partner with and also, limit your team size. Usually too few is superior to too many but proper count should be established for each individual locale. Never take ten to a two story haunted farm house and conversely, don't take four members to a large cemetery. There are options to train personnel with outside sites and cemeteries where you can take many more people than the usual investigation. A site that fits all of these needs is the Paulding Light located in Paulding, Michigan near Watersmeet on the Wisconsin border. The Paulding Light is a mysterious phenomenon in the middle of the woods that has been investigated by many national television shows from *Ripley's Believe It or Not* to *Fact or*

Faked with absolutely no answer as to why this light glows or what it is.

Legends range from Native American Indian lore to a dead railroad brakeman. We once met a lady that had been visiting the Paulding Light for over eleven years, writing a book and working with a physicist on the "dip" and the extraordinary lights that occur there. She also alerted us to the Native American lore that abounds here.

The mysterious Paulding Light

It doesn't matter what the reason, the Paulding Light is there every night and offers a location that could tolerate 20 hunters with room for more. It is a pre-made training facility! More in the upcoming *UPST Case Study Digest*!

"What is that ringing?" I demanded.

The sky was overcast and through the fog, you could barely see the nose on your own face. Finding this small private cemetery was difficult, but the effort in being allowed to stand amongst these three small and well kept graves was rewarding if only for its pious setting.

Ding, ding, ding.

"I think it's my car," whispered Hillary.

Although miles off the traveled roads and deep in the woods on a two track trail, the hum of M-28 offered a haunting background that echoed an eerie din through the trees.

After disarming the car key alarm system we conducted an EVP recording session.

"Hi Amanda, my name is David." I began. "With me, as usual, is my son Christian and this lady is Professor Van Pels, **not** *Van Helsing, so don't worry about it."*

The Professor laughed as she slugged me in the left arm and the investigation continued.

– Trudell Cemetery Investigation, 12:30 am

5

Equipment Basics

kay, you are James Bond and I am Agent Q. It is my assignment to get you all the equipment necessary to complete your mission. I am going to tell you what you need to have and give you the condensed version of how it works and how to use it. I will even tell you where you can find it, get it cheap or even make it. There are some simple things I call *Life Savers* that every team should start with. I will cover these now before we break down the specifics of paranormal equipment.

- Proper Clothes: Dress warmly and properly.
- Food and Water: Bring extra for energy.
- Cell phone.
- Flashlight.
- First aid kit

Chapter 5

First of all, dress appropriately. Warm clothes in layers can always be removed. Our team also carries chemical hand warmers. They are cheap and can be used over and over again. Wear a hat. My problem is always the basement joists while looking at my Infrared Thermometer. BEWARE THE HEAD BUTT! Those won't be ghosts you are seeing... they will be stars! In fact, if you are taller than the norm, I recommend you always wear a ball cap. It doesn't keep you from hitting your noggin, but it definitely provides some protection. Proper footwear is also important as cold feet make a cold person which cools enthusiasm. More hunts are ended by cold feet than by exhaustion. Don't forget rain gear and umbrellas if it is an outside hunt. A raincoat covers your body, but an umbrella covers your equipment.

Bring extra food and water. Energy bars are good to quell an appetite and lift your productivity in the wee hours of the morning. Of course, your team can carry their drinks, but I recommend taking a five minute time out when you discern the energy level of the team dipping. This is important especially in an inside location. You don't want your team stumbling around in the dark with a spillable drink.

Another important item for the team to carry is a cellular telephone. You never know when it may come in handy but not everyone needs to or should carry their cell phone. Be sure to turn the phone off during the investigation, especially when conducting EVP work or using an EMF detector. Turn it on only in an emergency; yes, your detector may pick up your cell phone.

Always carry a first aid kit. Make sure it has the necessities like band aids, antiseptic, additional field dressing and a pain reliever of some kind. You may want to carry some additional items like anti-histamines and even smelling salts and anti-diuretics; seriously. Although it is very likely that your kit will never be opened, you shouldn't hunt without it. So, before you even leave your house, be sure to have the above.

Since there is so much specific equipment to cover, I think it best that we break the items down into different chapters. What you are reading now covers Basic & Inexpensive Essentials. Since these are the necessities that you will need before you even step out of your house, they will be arranged on basis of priority. The next chapters will outline Advanced but Affordable Gear, and Luxury Equipment along with Traditional Favorites. These chapters will not be ordered in ay particular fashion so they will actually have to be read, reviewed and not retrieved. We start with the Basic Essentials:

- **Storage trunk**

I start with this item because as you acquire equipment, rather than having it strewn about the house, it is best to have it localized in one place. I recommend going to a second hand store like Goodwill or St. Vincent De Paul's to acquire a large trunk with a handle. You may even have one in your attic or garage. The major discount stores also sell plastic trunks. They are lighter but they can get pricey. Storage bins will also work, but I feel a trunk with a handle is easier to move and provides better protection for any fragile equipment inside. The other nice part is that paint sticks better to metal and wood. You can paint the trunk with your team colors, telephone number and logo. (Your children will find this great fun). You will further want to create alternate compartments within the trunk to categorize and inventory equipment. I made these out of empty candy containers from a grocery store but you can use anything that you may find; even simple cardboard boxes. When labeled, this will make the Tech Managers inventory duties much easier. Remember that any money you don't spend on frivolous items like individual storage containers can be put into equipment that you can actually use on an investigation.

- **Flashlight**

One of the very first pieces of equipment an investigator should carry is obviously the flashlight. As a seasoned investigator you will discover that the only light source you will want, if any, is a flashlight. This is important for seeing where you are walking as well as monitoring your equipment read-outs. Something else I recommend for your flashlight is a red lens. A red lens is much better in the dark as it takes off the edge of the non-filtered bulb and is easier on the eyes. If your flashlight comes with an extra lens, great! If not I recommend your going to a craft store where you will find sheets of colored plastic. Making a red filter is cheaper than buying a lens and is also very simple to install on your flashlight. Remove the lens, trace it on the plastic, cut it out and then put it between the casing and the lens. Be sure not to place the plastic filter between the lens and the bulb as it can get warm in there with extended use.

I should mention other flashlight functions that may surprise you. Using a flashlight as a way to communicate with a disembodied entity is also coming back into vogue. Many investigators, while conducting EVP sessions, will lay a flashlight in a remote place, but within their view. They will have already unscrewed the top casing, leaving it loose enough to allow the flashlight to turn on and off with a touch. Asking questions like "if you are there, can you turn on the light for me" sometimes elicits astounding results.

I should also mention multi use flashlights. These inexpensive and long lasting flashlights have different settings including UV and laser along with an LED illuminating light. Every team should carry at least one.

Individuals should carry their own flashlight but try to limit the light to one primary user per group. This is to be used only when absolutely necessary and only by others if they feel insecure in their footing. They mess with the IR LEDs. If you want a light show go to Las Vegas. Bring extra batteries and extra flashlights. One last thing: popular theory is that spirit activity creates a drain on anything electronic (batteries). You will learn that when conducting a paranormal investigation, your batteries run down unusually fast. Always bring extra batteries and flashlights.

- **Digital Camera**

Digital Camera

The affordable digital camera may be the one tool that has really brought paranormal investigation to the masses. The digital camera is great for night and day hunts, unlimited in photos (depending on your memory card), and most importantly, after initial purchase very inexpensive to view and download. Some even take video! As far as quality, most digitals give you options like good, better, and best that relate to memory and dpi used. In fact, digital quality can be comparable to all but the very best of film cameras. So you have a digital camera and let's say 500 pictures to take, what do you do? Well it depends on the investigation, but simple rule of thumb. The more photos you take the more chance you have of catching something. Here are a few reasons to take more digital pictures.

1. **Snapshot Chronicle**: You establish a photographic account of every investigation. Pictures of people taking part, locale, and equipment etc. All may come in handy when authenticating or recollecting an investigation. Some teams forget to take photos of the other members of their squad, instead focusing on dark corners or antique furniture. Don't forget the team! It is important to know who was where and when. In addition, often activity occurs around human beings so let the photos rip.

2. **Random documentation**: Many believe that if you shoot a random area that appears empty, when you look at the picture something may show up in your photo. Everything from orbs to mists to non-corporeal entities may appear. This is especially useful while conducting EVP sessions.

3. **Pre and Post photography**. In many investigations, inanimate objects are believed to have moved. We at the UPST have adopted the strategy of taking walk through photographs of these active locations and then post-hunt photos from the same angle that document the movement or lack thereof.

   An original twist that the UPST employs in pre and post hunt photography is what we call "Ghost Traps."

Basically this is a pre-made diagram that allows the investigator to measure actual movement.

For instance, one of these boards looks like a bullseye or target and the other a cross hair (these will be offered in the appendix with this book for your duplication). These traps can be employed in any number of ways. We use them for tracking the movement of objects that have been known to kinetically travel and to monitor movement while conducting EVP  with intelligent spirits. In other words, placing a marble or a Tonka toy on one of these charts and asking: "if you can hear me, can you move this object?" Pre and post digital photographs have paid off many times for the UPST! More on this in specialty tools.

The last word on digital cameras as with all electronic gear is this: bring extra batteries! Batteries are easy to find, but it's hard to find a full body apparition. When you analyze your photos look for anything out of the ordinary or for items that don't match your pre-hunt photos. Remember that 99% of what you catch on camera can be explained. Analysis may be long and mundane but be skeptical. For instance, orbs can most times be debunked as dust, insects, etc. but they are still fun. I recommend you take many pictures and examine them; use this important tool and in fact, take hundreds of photos. Push the limit of your memory card. Digital photos that show nothing are easily deleted at no cost. The chance that you catch something on record is priceless.

- **Notepad & clipboard** w/pencils and log sheets.

It's a good idea to back up all evidence or personal experience with "hard copy" or written record. Evidence like photos, video and audio cannot possibly validate every incident and if you capture media, it should be considered the "frosting on the cake." You will be surprised at how much quicker you get through the information when you have some old fashioned paper sitting in front of you.

Included with this book is access to a Log Form which your team can personalize, use during the hunt and particularly after every group sweep. Items pertinent to an investigation such as squads, assignments and gear allocation should be logged. Any incident should be recorded in the log whether or not it is believed that your camera recorded the event. Take five minutes between new partners to log what you have experienced or not experienced with your last. Be as specific as possible with time, locations and incident. Your team leader and analysts will find this information invaluable in retracing evidence. Always bring along extra forms, pens, and pencils; colored marker pens also come in handy.

- **Watch**

A watch is important for a number of reasons and not limited to just keeping time. It doesn't hurt to announce the time on almost every occasion you speak during an investigation. The analyst reviewing a video of this practice will thank you kindly. Another nifty function of the watch is if it has a "stop-watch" built into it. With sounds, lights or other seemingly paranormal occurrence, regularity and duration can be measured. For instance, in a house where you are experiencing a knock every forty-five seconds, is the regularity indicative of a hot water boiler in the basement, the house settling or something more. Another example documented by the UPST was at the Paulding Light, where we measured the duration of the light for up to three minutes and forty-five seconds. We easily debunked the "car light" theory because the time and straight stretch in a car going an average 55 on US-45 simply doesn't add up to a three minute forty-five second continuous reflection. We will talk more about this investigation later in the upcoming *UPST Case Study Digest*. Needless to say, a watch and stop-watch are cheap necessities, especially if they are one and the same.

- **Compass**

A compass is a cheap and multi-functional instrument useful to any team for more than just direction on an outside hunt, (spirits often alter normal magnetic fields). They are small, easily found and inexpensive. A compass with a light can be purchased for under $10. You may even have one in your drawer. We all know that compasses pick up and point toward magnetic north and this function is what makes this tool helpful in a paranormal investigation. Some believe that the compass goings-on described within the Bermuda and Great Lakes Triangles demonstrate the same electrical magnetic disturbance you will be attempting to capture. When using your compass on an investigation check it immediately when entering the location and make sure that it is reading correctly with pointer north. When your compass needle wobbles or spins this is indicative of an electro magnetic disturbance. A compass can be carried or located within sight if you are conducting an EVP recording session. It will occasionally even beat the EMF detector in tracking a disturbance in the electro magnetic field.

- **Dowsing Rods**

These tools are sometimes referred to as Divining Rods and are a low cost tool that almost all paranormal investigators still swear by. I recommend every team have a set or two, especially due to their inexpensive nature. The dowsing or divining rods are usually constructed from a

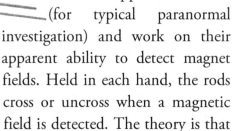

metal like copper or brass (for typical paranormal investigation) and work on their apparent ability to detect magnet fields. Held in each hand, the rods cross or uncross when a magnetic field is detected. The theory is that

Dowsing Rods

when a spirit or entity is present the entity alters ambient energy which can be measured by tools such as EMF detectors, K2 meters and of course Dowsing Rods. Although for use in paranormal investigations these rods are usually constructed from metals, for other uses they are simply wooden. Old timers in the Midwest, when preparing to drill water wells, would call their friend who could "witch" for water with wooden divining rods. These wooden rods, sometimes actually shaped more like a wishbone, would steer the "witcher" to the water.

Using the dowsing rods is as simple as holding them steadily but loosely in your hands and walking. It does take the proper touch to allow the rods to move fluidly within your hands but this is easily mastered. The reason that I recommend copper or brass for paranormal investigation is that metal seems to be less sensitive to bodies of water and more sensitive to the electro magnetic disturbance innate in a hunt. If your dowsing rods cross you can infer from the speed of the movement as to the strength of the activity. Additionally, when using dowsing rods, a good practice is to have another team member carrying an EMF detector to join you and verify your detection with their readings.

- **Digital Thermometer**

The digital thermometer can be an inexpensive substitute and back up for the more advanced Infrared (IR) Thermometer described later in this chapter, but it does have a place of its own. A digital thermometer actually measures ambient temperature where as an infrared thermometer measures the temperature of a surface. The standard digital thermometer usually comes with a remote probe and can be switched from Fahrenheit to Celsius. Theory dictates that a spirit manifests through the gathering of energy (heat or cold) which is 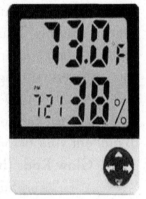 measurable. A digital thermometer although not displaying immediate results (like the IR Thermometer) can still be useful if a cold spot event is extended or permanent. Immediately take a base reading and if the temperature varies by 5-10 degrees, you may have some activity. Inside and for standard digital thermometers, the UPST employs our **5 and 10 Sense Rule** in minutes: If an investigator notices a minimum average 5 degree temperature drop sustained over 10 minutes there is likely activity or a minimum average rise of 5 degrees over 10 minutes, there was likely activity. A digital thermometer is also useful in monitoring the results you gather with your IR Thermometer.

- **Barometer**

A Barometer is a common gauge like tool that measures rise and fall in barometric pressure. A barometer is sometimes labeled with such general classifications as "rain" "clear," etc. This can be very helpful in outdoor hunts such as cemeteries. In addition to being tied to weather, some believe that when manifesting itself, a spirit may cause an increase or decrease of barometric pressure. When using a barometer during an investigation, first take a base or control reading. This means record the initial barometric pressure when you arrive at the location and compare it as you progress through the hunt. Usually a change in millibars (mb) of 20 or more is indicative of extraordinary or paranormal turmoil. Don't wait until something occurs to pull out your barometer and be sure to log your results.

- **Glow Rods (bracelets, necklaces, etc.)**

Super cheap addition to your storage trunk and the kids will love em'! These are those little glow in the dark illuminators that can be formed into the bracelets and necklaces that you see the children wearing around on Halloween. These inexpensive little gems come in great on all investigations, but are especially valuable on outside hunts like large cemeteries, or multiple location venues as they are not bright enough to disturb an investigation but still allow visual identification of your team. In other words, they allow you to see and know who you are looking at in complete dark (most come in color). Pick them up at the dollar store at ten for a few dollars!

- **Tripod**

You can find an inexpensive tripod anywhere from a garage sale to goodwill to online. When I say inexpensive, I don't mean cheap. A good quality tripod can be obtained inexpensively and will last forever if it is of sufficient quality. These are a necessity for every paranormal team with a video camera and can be of additional use with 35mm, digital cameras, motion sensors, lasers, etc. Be sure to spend the extra few dollars to get one that is adjustable up and down a couple of feet. The allure of the less expensive desktop models although sometimes useful should be avoided. Of course, they don't take up much room and can be used for static shots in hallways, on graves, etc., but the double duty extension tripod can fulfill these same functions along with many others.

Christian contributes to the poor box at a dilapidated church in Ohio-An effort to elicit activity.

"*Don't you hear that?*" Tania insisted.

I knew my hearing wasn't first-class, so I refocused my frustration into total silence. The hallway of the old hotel stretched out endlessly in front of us. Twenty doors if there were one. We hunched silently in the hallway not moving, not breathing, but listening.

"*I hear it!*" whispered Christian, "*Music?*"

"*Ssusssshhhh!!!!*" I instructed my son.

And suddenly there it was. A music... low and whirling within many voices... maybe a party? ... a movie? ... from above...
"*but Ed told us there was nobody on the third floor,*" I said.

– House of Ludington, April 26, 2009, 2:34 am

6

Advanced Gear

M uch of the equipment listed in this chapter might be considered essential by some but don't forget that "ghost hunting" has been practiced for a thousand years and long before most of this stuff was even invented. I am not anti-gear, but I am pro-smarts. This means that an experienced paranormal investigator with a flashlight and a digital camera will be more successful than a newbie with an EMF detector and a Thermal imager in every hunt. Keep this in mind when equipping your team. Be sure to take slow steady steps before you run to buy advanced and experienced gear:

- **Two-way Radio**

Two-way radios are the primary external form of communication we use in the UPST. As you have already discovered, I frown on cell phones for other reasons, but let's talk about the good points of two-ways: instant communication, acknowledgement of phenomena, updates and direction. There are many different brands of two-ways and the UPST has worked with all of them; most are adequate to good. When purchasing a two-way, look only for the models that have multiple channels, usually from 1-22. This allows the radio to interact with the parallel frequencies of other brands. Some reach miles away.

In the United States, there are two different sets of frequencies on typical 22 channel radios. One is open to free public use and the other to FCC licensed use. In other words, one is reserved for "Family Radio Service" and the other for "General Mobile Radio Service." You can use FRS frequencies without a license and these are channels 1-14. Channels 1-7 require a hybrid radio which lowers non-commercial (FRS) wattage on these channels to .5 watts as they are also sometimes used for official use or law enforcement. Channels 1 and 3 are often used by local law enforcement, so stay away from these.

Licensed use is "required" on the GMRS, channels 15-22. The reason that I have put required in quotes is that it is unlikely that if you use these channels you will ever be identified. Many two-ways are found on Channel 19, which is known as the trucking channel and I have found that if asked for their call number or FCC license, many opt not to respond; but activity on these channels does tend to irritate licensed operators using them legally. Although as an American I believe the air is free, ultimately, I recommend channels 8-14 as optimum with the exception of 11 and 14 which are still used for children's short range walkie talkies.

You don't want a child's voice whispering out at night asking "is anyone there?" That means 8, 9, 10, 12, and 13. Don't allow your squads to choose their own channels as we have found this disruptive to communication. I wanted to see if you were paying attention…☺

Here are a few tips that the UPST has learned through the school of hard knocks. First, when communicating with a two-way, be sure to engage the talk or transmit button a split second before you speak. You will find that this will include your whole statement as the transmitter does not engage with your trigger simultaneously. When operating with multiple two-ways, the communication should always be initiated with a call to the team leader. This eliminates team talk over. Let me give you an example of a hunt conversation that occurred at an outside location:

Investigator 1: "Hey David… are you there."

Lead: "Yeah Joe."

Investigator 1: "Did Bryson's team find that grave yet, because I don't see a light where they were heading to."

Lead: "Bryson… did you find that grave and where are you at?"

Investigator 2: "No, we didn't, but we're looking over near that fountain thing…. I can see your light Joe"

Investigator 1: "Cool… when are we wrapping this up?"

Lead: "45 minutes… find that grave Brys… Out"

Investigator 1: "Over and out."

Investigator 2: "yeah, out."

What you just read is a conversation that covered proper protocol in counting on the team leader to monitor conversation. This is important for many different reasons such as allowing the team and the team leader to know your locale, movements and plan. By including the leader as the monitor of the conversation, you assure no talk over, and everyone hears details and outcome. If you have a base station, the base operator may take the lead in communication at the leader's discretion.

Another practice we have found useful is noise acknowledgment. In other words, if you make a noise, like dropping a tool that may be heard by another team member, let them know. The phrase: "That noise was Jim dropping his flashlight on the second floor" may save someone asking, getting excited or recording and celebrating a non paranormal experience.

Some people believe that on occasion two-way radios will intermittently pick up non corporeal communication… another plus! Take this type of activity with a grain of salt as all these channels are open to the public.

Although most two-ways are designed to reach over many miles, don't be overly concerned if you have difficulty in communication. There are many causes for lowered range including electro magnetic interference, obstructions like trees and hills, low batteries, etc. For instance, on our Paulding Light investigation, which will be explored in the upcoming *UPST Case Studies Digest*, several of the above issues hindered our two-way use: trees, hills and electro magnetic disturbances galore. In addition to most of the investigation being directly beneath a high tension power cable, much of the actual phenomena seemed to be electrical in nature. This type of activity is definitely not copasetic to two-way use, but don't get frustrated. You will have to use a different form of contact on this type of investigation. Here are some tips: Try to set semi-rigid time tables. In other words if communication fails, expect to meet with the other group at a particular time. Of course, if any group is experiencing activity, this rule goes out the window. The second form of contact is visual and you should create your own flashlight signals with your team. We base our signals around Morse code, with blinks lasting one second and dashes or pauses lasting about double that. These are a few of the signals that the UPST use:

- Attention (are you there?): wave the flashlight above your head back and forth.
- Yes: One flash.
- No: Two flashes.
- Experienced something: Three flashes.
- Ready to come in (swing): Four flashes.
- Come in: Wave as in "attention" and four flashes.
- Circle: Everything is OK.
- Help, come here: 3 blinks, 3 dashes, 3 blinks (SOS).

You will find that instead of turning your flashlight off and on, the better method is in simply covering the end of it with your hand to indicate your signal and then turning it off after your message awaiting a response. This becomes fun as your team starts to add its own code and you will find that your use of two-ways will diminish somewhat in outdoor settings adding to the silence that is a boon to all paranormal investigations.

- **35 MM Camera**

If you own a 35 millimeter camera, you may find that it will come in handy for particular applications in your investigation. 35mm cameras have fallen into disrepute since the advent and subsequent popularity of digital cameras. Of course, the digital camera pros become glaringly apparent when addressing the traditional 35mm cons. First of all, a standard SLR (single lens reflex) 35mm requires film. This must be purchased and later developed. This can be pricey and does not allow immediate analysis that you may need or prefer on an investigation. Another point to consider is the limited photo picture capacity. A 35mm, depending on film, will take a quantity in the low double digits whereas with a digital, the quantity is limited only by the memory you purchase. Also, a 35mm (unless with auto-focus) is not particularly handy in the dark and of course, the download of photos is more difficult.

So why take a 35mm, even if you have one? I for one, at times, prefer the unpredictability and sometimes superiority of photos taken with a 35mm. Different film and filters can be used that accentuate different light spectrums such as infrared and ultraviolet range. Some believe that exploring these invisible light bands may lead to an occasional shot of something hiding within them. The fact that these anomalies cannot be altered as easily as with digital media is also a pro.

Another interesting function a good 35mm can perform is called Time Lapse Photography. This allows the investigator to shoot in nearly total darkness by slowing the shutter speed. This offers two different photographic tricks: First, photos taken with a slow shutter lighten the room appearing as though in night vision, and secondly it also retards any moving object displaying a blur of action. Any time lapse photography must be done with a tripod and remote trigger to limit camera shake. As for the film to use on an investigation, I recommend using at least 400 speed film and 800-1000 outdoors. Final word on 35mm? Not necessary, but not obsolete. Never limit your tools.

• **Audio Recorders**

Audio recorders are another very important tool for your paranormal team. I recommend your team carrying at least one to back up your video camera and to expound upon it. There are two different types of audio recorders. Analog and Digital with variations, one of which I will cover; the RT (Real Time) recorder:

1. **Analog** - First is the analog tape recorder. Okay, I know what you are thinking. Those went out with 8-tracks didn't they? Quick answer: Yes, and find one if you can. Analog recorders offer you built in white noise which theoretically assists EVP or electronic voice phenomena in more readily manifesting. You can find an analog cassette tape recorder in your garage, Ebay or even at Goodwill. Reel to reel, although higher quality is too bulky, go with cassette. Use high biased tape and an external microphone to cut down on the sound of the unit itself. The microphone should  be unidirectional for close areas and Omni-directional for larger applications. If not a handheld recorder, sit the microphone and unit in one place and let the tape roll.

2. **Digital** – Digital tape recorders come in different digital formats such as DAT, WAV, Mp3, etc. Mp3 is the most popular format and is easily

found in most electronic stores and online. The convenience of an mp3 recorder is due in part to longer recording time and ease of download. It has nearly forced the analog recorder into retirement. These recorders are small, light and can be carried with ease. They are equally adept with either EVP work or left in a suspect location as a blind monitor. In addition to zero tape cost, digital media is easier to download, easier to organize as computer files rather than tapes, and easier to review.

3. **Real Time EVP Recorder** – New to paranormal investigation is this cute little trick that employs a time buffer that allows nearly instant review of electronic voice phenomena. This, in effect, allows the investigator to actually communicate with whatever entity might be attempting to be heard in near real time. Although a bit pricey, if you have the money, not a bad investment.

When using any recorder always conduct a lead in. State your name; introduce your team, location, date and time. I like my investigators to do this every time they turn their recorder or cam on and off. Always log any time that you believe something odd or out of place may have been picked up by your recorder for ease in analysis. Make sure your analysts are patient people as every hour of media may yield that rare second of paranormal evidence.

• **Electro Magnetic Field Detector (EMF)**
Electro Magnetic field detectors (EMF detector) or cell sensors are without a doubt one of the more popular paranormal tools in use today! The

good part is that in being such, pricing has dropped drastically. Of course by now you are familiar with the ideology behind tracking electro magnetic disturbances on paranormal investigations. EMFs are at the top of the heap for detecting this type of activity.

If the team owns the EMF detectors, disperse them one to a group. Try not to have more than one per group unless using the second is only to verify the readings of the first. More than one leads to a team breaking up as each follows there own analogous signal. Contrary to other "experts" you may have read, I do not recommend heading out on your own looking for electro magnetic signal. At the UPST we use the buddy rule for all investigation steps other than lockdown, which will be discussed in detail later. There are two reasons for this rule: First, it is best to work in a group so that your team accomplishes their objectives and logs the results expeditiously. Secondly, if you do get EMF readings or have a personal experience, it is always best to have your buddy along to verify the event. Be sure that your results have not occurred when you are standing near an electrical outlet, power line, appliance or circuit box as all of these create electro magnetic fields. Some EMF detectors manuals list many appliances and the corresponding readings. In addition, you will find your own investigative tools also affect your EMF detector: cell phones, video cameras, etc. We have experienced an amazing connectivity between the EMF and two-way radios, in fact, up to 20 feet away. Test and re-test your results. If you get a reading, your EMF detector is likely to emit lights and sound with increasing speed the stronger the signal, attempt to locate the source of the emission. Every EMF has its own scale of measurement and different paranormal groups suggest that a reading between 1.5 and 8.0 is indicative of paranormal activity. I recommend you throw these strict parameters in the garbage can. The UPST has documented activity when the EMF has been dead, and had no personal experiences when it has been off the scale. I recommend, as with all measuring gear, you run a baseline control check through your location before starting the investigation and periodically log all the results.

- **Infrared Thermometer**

 Infrared Thermometers have become an important item in every paranormal tool box. They are reasonably priced and very useful if even just for measuring normal conditions on an isolated and cold hunt. A thermal scanning tool allows the investigator to measure object temperatures from a remote point. In other words, they can become a detection system for paranormal activity manifestation, usually indicated by a quick temperature drop. The theory is that a spirit needs energy to subsist, thus gathering energy (heat or cold) which causes measurable localized temperature alteration.

I recommend that your team carry at least a non-laser unit which is vision blind and if you can afford it, also a laser model which is a bit more expensive. Don't spend over 35 dollars on the former or 80 dollars on the latter. Prices continue to fall and I have noted some laser units on Ebay for under $20.00. If your readout is not illuminated, carry a flashlight so that you can see the readings. Establish your base temperature and state your results out loud for your group videographer. Monitor the readout visually with a video camera when possible. Also, be sure to log your results in your team's field report. The UPST applies the **5**

and 10 Sense Rule in seconds: If an investigator notices a 5 degree drop in 10 seconds there <u>is</u> likely activity or a rise of 5 degrees in 10 seconds, there <u>was</u> likely activity. Remember, the infrared thermometer does not collect ambient temperatures, but the surface of its target INSTANTLY. This has been extremely helpful for my team in the past when, on more than one occasion, an investigator thought that they had been touched on the shoulder. I immediately compared temperature shoulder to shoulder and noted a 17 degree temperature variable. More than a 10 degree differential is rare but possible and thank goodness I documented this event on video.

The UPST has created one double duty trick that you may employ with an infrared thermometer with laser. Many investigators believe that when a laser beam is projected into a room or area in which paranormal activity is occurring, an actual entity will break the beam. So when you are randomly using your infrared thermometer, be sure to note the continuation of your laser beam. If this technique is successful for you, you may want to move on to a professional laser which I outline next.

- **Laser Grid**

As described above, theory dictates that a random laser beam can be broken by an entity crossing it. Moving up to a pro laser used for DJ or light show work may be a

little pricy but you'll be pleasantly surprised at how little a light duty laser costs. These upscale lasers allow you to vary and set individual beams in wide patterns that run automatically sideways up and down or statically. If the pattern is wide enough and running a cross pattern, you may actually be able to view the outline of an entity. The laser unit can be set up on a piece of furniture or preferably on a tripod. The laser is useful in EVP sessions or to monitor an empty room with a static camera. Use the laser in as total darkness as you can create, and always use an approved personal unit for eye safety. Locate your video camera behind the laser and pointed at the spread pattern. Make sure your camera has either lowlight or night shot on so that you can better make out the pattern and experiment first. Do not waste your money on small handheld lasers; they are gimmicks.

- **Low Frequency Monitor**

Almost everybody has an old walkie talkie, a baby monitor or a hand held AM radio. Toss it in your box and leave it within ear shot running static and let it roll. Some have documented spirit voices over these cheap and easily attainable devices. They also create a natural white noise if you use this method with your team. Another plus is that when hunting with children, this gives them useful tool which they can carry that actually performs a function.

- **Motion Sensor**

We are all familiar with the concept of a motion sensor or detector, you know, the little box hanging on the wall that triggers a light or alarm when you wave your arms. Some believe that these units not only sense simple movement, but can react to moving cold spots that might manifest with the presence of a spirit. Many investigators swear by them. I take the "couldn't hurt" stance, especially when on a  large hunt when your team has been stretched by low numbers. Some motion sensors come with a remote receiver that will allow you to know when the unit was triggered without sound. This receiver should be carried with you.

The Family Guide to Ghost Hunting

Set up the sensor in a hallway, near an active door or even with a battery operated model at a grave of interest. Of course, if the detector goes off in the middle of the investigation, send a group loaded for bear. A motion detector is another affordable tool for the paranormal investigator. You may even have one in your garage or know where you can get one very cheaply. Another great accessory with some motion sensors is a remote off keychain. If the unit goes off, you can turn it off from a different location. I have seen these particular units priced under $20.00 for up to 25 feet. Excellent to sit in front of a door that opens by itself after the team settles in for the night. The paranormal investigator's tool box has many compartments so be sure they are filled.

- **Power wand**

A Power wand is basically a no bells and whistles EMF also referred to as a Ground Sensor. This little tool comes in handy during an investigation, even if just shoved in your back pocket awaiting a trip near the basement circuit breakers. When using this little baby in an investigation all the same rules regarding electro magnetic qualities of spirits apply. Most of these wands have a button on them that you hold and point and release. If the wand lights up, you have picked up an electro magnetic disturbance (usually an ungrounded or older electrical system) or perhaps an "entity?" As with all sensing equipment attempt to locate the source of the signal remember to log your results and announce them for your videographer and alert other team groups about the reading.

- **Specialty Items**

Specialty items are things that you bring to a hunt specific to the research and history regarding said investigation. For instance, in locations that manifest kinesis in inanimate objects moving, the UPST employs their Ghost Traps with objects like marbles, toys and even cigars. A couple of examples: Captain Joseph Willy Townshend who haunts the Seul Choix Point Lighthouse enjoys inspecting and moving cigars. We brought English Coronas to the hunt and sat them on a Cross-Hair Ghost Trap to be photographically monitored. Another logical extension of using specialty items was to bring my son Christian's wooden trains whistle to the Paulding Light. The experience here is built upon the legend of a dead railroad brakeman. I have to admit that when some drunken college kids arrived to check out the phenomena, Christian's train whistle received many shocked expressions. Doing the proper history research should alert your team to what and if to include specialty items in your investigation.

- **Video camera**

A video camera preferably with infrared capability should be a staple of every equipment manifest. If flashlights are the first weapon of the paranormal investigator, perhaps IR video cameras are the "shock and awe." Anyway, my team agrees that they are, at the very least, the most fun! Beyond their obvious qualities, like documenting all aspects of an investigation, video cameras add much more. One of these is a personal connection between the investigation and your team which instigates a professionalism sometimes not occurring without recording.

Video cameras come in many different formats. In addition to DV (digital video) cameras, which record on tape, newer cameras actually come with their own hard drive. With technology prices dropping everyday these hard drive units, which are in effect a mini-computer, have become very affordable.

Video camera qualities include:

1. **Investigation Documentation** – Video cameras provide reviewable evidence that an investigation not only occurred, but when, and who participated.

2. **Phenomena Record** – Your camera creates a media record of what the human eye can and cannot see. In addition, your camera records not only everything in front of it, but everything within range of its microphone. Never forget EVP (electronic voice phenomena) can be recorded by cameras as well as recorders.

3. **Infrared Capability** – In effect, this video camera option allows you to see in the dark (or near total darkness). Initially I had vowed not to promote brand names, but in the case of video cameras, it cannot be helped. When you go out to purchase your video camera, look for a Sony. Sony Night Shot provides one infrared LED on your camera which illuminates total darkness within a range of a few feet. Additional remote infrared lighting can be purchased to extend your range exponentially. The night shot function included on Sony video cameras is second to none. In fact, if you check out most paranormal television shows, you will see what they use from the name on the hand band. I will get into where and how to buy this product later.

4. **Static Shot** – Many haunts have a particular location that is invariably the focal point of kinetic activity. In other words, objects move. The UPST has gotten into

the habit of setting a static video overnight at these locales. Static shots require your camera to be held motionless for hours. Of course you can sit the camera on a piece of furniture, but your better option is an inexpensive tripod as I mentioned earlier. With a tripod, proper height and angle are more easily achieved. We at the UPST have reviewed up to 64 hours of static video from one investigation. It can be painstaking, but can also be very rewarding as in the investigation of the Fayette Historic State Park.

5. **Phasing** – This is a technique invented by the UPST upon the advent of infrared video several years ago. Many paranormal investigators, including myself, have questioned the new and total reliance upon infrared cameras. In many investigations, I have relied on shadows and peripheral vision as personal experience demonstrative of paranormal activity. Infrared night vision tends to limit shadows and obscure the potential radiant energy of manifestations. To make up for this deficiency in infrared cameras, the UPST created a technique that we refer to as phasing. Although not for use in total darkness, in subdued lighting, it works like this: Basically there is a repeated toggling from on to off of the night shot function in an effort to catch what the human eye alone can and cannot see. Announce your intention to phase so that the audio of your camera picks it up and your analysts know what they are looking at. The shifting should be regular at about 5-10 second intervals which will give the camera time to focus on the differing light levels. Shoot uncharacteristic sections of the room or spot you are in intermittently or directly at an area any time you sense something unseen.

Video cameras come with different sizes, shapes and features. Night shot is great, but not absolute and the more running video the better. Always have a back up battery and be prepared to run a good 4 hours of video on even a half-night investigation. A Sony with night shot capability and 60 gigabytes of memory (20 hours plus) can now be purchased for under $300 dollars. I recommend Amazon.com as a good starting place for reasonable pricing. After getting an idea as to price, you may want to shop your local dealer, Amazon or Ebay and get a deal. Go cheap, go warrantee.

• **White Noise**

White Noise is the sound that you hear on television or radio stations that are not quite tuned in. It is also a tool that early EVP experts relied on to help manifest disembodied voices. Analog tape recorders, as you have read earlier create their own white noise, but you can bring your own canned white noise along for an investigation. The theory is that because white noise fills all sound frequencies, it can be easily used by entities to produce electronic voice phenomena. The down side is that the white noise sometimes has the tendency to obscure other relevant sounds like tapping, knocking or even investigator voices. A decent graphic or parametric equalizer can be used to effectively filter out excess noise during analysis and it is also easily accomplished with most digital audio software.

"Will an ax head work?"

Melissa, of the UPST and the Iron County Paranormal squad, looked toward the car inquisitively as she searched through the back of her truck.

"Let me try it," Rob spoke in a restraint tempered by frustration.

Paranormal investigations often involve challenges in excess of simply finding strange phenomena. In this case, an outside investigation with a key locked inside the car.

"Here, try this!" Joe said as he jogged from the UPST storage trunk.

Rob looked at the item, "Yeah that might work."

I walked over to see if the guys had been successful in opening the car and saw them working feverishly with a bent corkscrew like object.

"Hey! Are those my dowsing rods!?" I asked the guys incredulously.

– Paulding Light II Investigation, September 8, 2010, 9:35 pm

7

Luxury & Traditional Favorites

The luxury item is a piece of equipment that is the frosting on the cake. Of course, a team that owns a Thermal Imager will never leave home without it. On the other hand, if I owned a Porsche, I would never leave home without that either, but until then, I guess I will just drive my Honda Gold Wing, it gets me there.

Luxury Equipment:

- **Fuel Lantern**

The good ole propane lantern is important for every paranormal team. Not every location that your team investigates will have electricity. As you will note later in the book, the UPST investigated the Helmer House Inn during the winter and with no electricity. The lantern is an invaluable piece of equipment, not only providing a continuous form of light for the equipment table, but a form of heat for our hands. Another application that the Coleman has shown itself useful is in our many cemetery and outside investigations. Depending on the graveyard, a central location may not be on a path or roadway and the propane lantern establishes an equipment distribution and meeting point that can be seen from a half a mile away. The propane lantern is surely a luxury, but one you may have in your garage.

- **Frank's Box or Spirit Box**

Sometimes referred to as a Ghost Box, Frank's Box was

invented by Frank Sumpton. It receives all frequencies on one crystal diode scanning across the AM or FM spectrums. Sumpton believes that spirit phenomena, such as EVP, can be caught in this limitless scanning process, most often in the AM radio frequency and his machine allows the investigator to experience EVP in real time. In other words, it allows the hunter to converse with spirits and not have to listen later. With updates, the "ghost box" can now allow specific AM frequencies to be isolated based on their results at a location. Frank's box has shown amazing results in forwarding paranormal communication but is a bit pricey if you're looking to simply expand your tool box: (think Germanium Diode).

Another claimed advancement in the area of real time EVP work comes through the "Spirit Box." These little units are more affordable and are gaining a great deal of popularity due to their use on paranormal television shows. Most sweep both the FM & AM frequency with similar results produced by "Frank's Box." This is a nice luxury tool at just over $100; A bit pricey? I can give you a hint though. Ebay has reasonable buys on Spirit or Ghost boxes and you can also make them (i.e. Radio Shack). Check out Youtube and Ebay for instructions and manuals.

- **Gas Detectors**

This can be a handy tool to have along on special investigations. Although the use may not justify the cost, there are unusual situations where this tool may be just what the paranormal investigation calls for. For instance, in our Seul Choix Point investigation, it is thought that the ghost that haunts the lighthouse likes cigars as this was his habit in life, and cigar smoke is often smelled at the site. Carbon monoxide from the smoke is something a gas detector will pick up. Another is the Paulding Light where some explanations of the light have been a form of swamp gas. A gas leak at a residential home can cause nausea. Gas detectors, much like a Geiger counter, allow the investigator to set a baseline and pick up several different forms of gas including possible methane or swamp gas. The other nice thing about this tool is that it can be used statically, in other words, sitting by itself. It is an audio device that speeds up its "beeps" as gas is detected. It is yet another luxury item for your toolbox.

- **Geiger Counter**

There are different types of Geiger Counters, but basically they all detect gamma radiation. The belief is that when a spirit or entity manifests itself it may give off some type of radiation. The Geiger counter is primarily an audio tool but does give readings, so some of the rules are different. Again with all types of metered equipment, do a baseline reading of your site. Most Geiger meters allow you to zero them out. This means you can adjust the base level to the natural reading of radiation at a particular location and your meter disallows it, only indicating "extra" readings (or unusual activity). A Geiger counter's unit of measurement is in rads per hour. Again our 1.5 rule comes into play when it may be encountering paranormal activity. Anything above 1.5 rads/hr is something to take note of.

- **GPS (Global Positioning System)**

This tool may be a bit pricey, but the UPST carries it because of the vast outside investigations that we conduct like the Paulding Light. A GPS uses an elaborate system of satellites that fix or triangulate your position sometimes within less than a meter. This is the same system that was developed to help the United States anti-ballistic cruise missiles attain an accuracy that is simply amazing. Now, it is in cars giving direction street by street. Quality handheld GPS units have visual screens that, after linking up, present the user with a map and their location. The more elaborate models allow you do download stored information from the GPS that will actually give you a visual track of your hunt. Not necessary, but nice.

- **Infrared Security DVR System**

You have all seen infrared security systems both on television and when you have been visiting Obama at his multi-million dollar Hawaiian vacation mansion (check out the image at the beginning of this chapter). Of course, the uses for a multi-camera infrared system are obvious. This technology, although not practical in the past, thanks to hard drive memory, has actually become very affordable over the past few years. These systems are based around "DVR" or Digital Video Recorder. Standard DVR systems have anywhere from a 250 to 1K gigabyte hard drive, with 4 to 8 Infrared cameras. This system not only allows the operation of all the static cameras simultaneously, it also splits the monitor screen into smaller views from each camera. Some teams don't like the wires that run from the cameras to the base, but we prefer these over wireless transmitters as they are more reliable for continuous signal. When you are probing into activities that elicit electro magnetic disturbances, you don't want to lose a signal when you need it to substantiate an experience. Hardwire is where it's at baby!

The other cool thing about an infrared security system with DVR is the ease of analysis. Fast motion, slow motion, scan features, hours of buffer time and the ease of pressing a button and burning it all to disc. Deliver a DVD disc to all the members of your team and ask them to analyze it. Spread the pain…☺.

• **Parabolic Listening Device**

A reverse cone-like structure that amplifies sound and this includes audio not heard by the human ear. This tool was originally designed for clandestine surveillance and you may have seen it being used in detective shows as a high-tech eavesdropper. In the paranormal field, the PLD comes in handy in almost all applications from EVP to just setting it up statically. Be sure you stick a recording device of some kind in line between the unit and your headphones. It would be a shame to hear a fantastic EVP and not be able to prove it. Some higher priced models have digital recorders built right in.

- **KII Meter**

The KII or K2 is yet another trendy form of electro magnetic detector. Due to its use on a popular television show, this detector has become the desire of many rookie investigators. They will spend exorbitant amounts of money to emulate their heroes. I actually met a team that had invested in a Thermal Imager before their first hunt. Needless to say, their pocketbook outweighed their passion and the team broke up and sold their FLIR camera with only 2 hunts under their belt. The good news is that the price on the K2 unit has dropped drastically, so don't pay over $60 dollars.

The K2 comes in handy for attempting communication with an entity while conducting an EVP (electronic voice phenomena) session. "Can you light this thing up?" is indicated immediately, and the K2 also serves the old "one for yes... two for no" scenario beautifully. Keep in mind that many less expensive EMF detectors do as well.

The K2 traditionally, has a button on the front of the meter which you press to enable the tool. You can disable this switch with a "slug" or a "penny" so the meter will run continuously, which is optimal. Some of the newer models have this option built in. If you find an older model just go to Youtube and search for "how to modify K2," and you will be walked through this process step by step. The UPST has achieved outstanding results with the less expensive cell sensor EMF detector which has a continuous function as well as a built in light. Measurement for the K2 is like all other EMF meters in milligaus (mg). Again, as with the above EMF detector, anything over 1.5mg should perk your interest but don't rely on any pre-set parameters from "experts" that you have observed or read. Any EMF detector is just a tool, not an absolute. When you buy the hammer don't consider the house built simply because you know that it can pound nails.

- **Night Vision Equipment**

Night vision equipment intensifies any light from an open window, the moon or stars or another piece of equipment. It can more prominently be aided by the use of Infrared Lighting. Night vision pricing has dropped drastically over the past five years. Of course you may already have a night vision camera, but additional night vision equipment, if within your budget, can be very helpful too. Some believe that infrared lighting actually illuminates spirits through reflected infrared light. We, at the UPST, do not believe this to be the case and believe that night vision simply helps the investigator see better in the dark. This may possibly better illuminate an entity that is difficult to see in more lighting, but that is all. We find this tool very helpful in most settings for a non-camera member. This teammate will not only keep your group from running into walls, but can aid the videographer in where to point if an incident is experienced. If your night vision member thinks that they see something be sure to log it and verify it with your other equipment.

One big negative of most night vision equipment (such as goggles) is they are cumbersome and burn batteries like crazy. Another is of course the price. Beware any tool; binoculars, camera, etc. that offers true night vision for $20 dollars. It's a rip off and although a nice gift for your child's birthday, it will not aid your team. The UPST, after much research, recommends the "Eyeclops" Night Vision Goggles system. This is a one eye unit that supplies actual and affordable infrared night vision. The only draw back is that it contains a small screen and only for one eye. We recommend keeping the other mobile eye hole open to cut down on the dizzying effect that occurs when moving with real night vision. There is no better deal in true night vision for under $100 dollars, and if you are patient, you can get them for even less! Watch Amazon and Ebay for good indicators on current price.

- **Obelisk**

Basically a tool that offers pre-programmed responses to audio signals (your voice). This piece of equipment can fall anywhere from creepy to stupid; Worth carrying for the price? No, but if your team has one, give it a try. It may surprise you and at least interest.

- **Tesla Coil**

The Tesla Coil was invented by Nikola Tesla in about 1891. In a nutshell, it creates electricity in the form of high voltage alternating current. You will be familiar with low power forms of this coil through films like Frankenstein or others that feature the "mad scientist." Although these coils are fragile and a bit exorbitant, they are still an amazing tool for any paranormal squad much like the laser described earlier. The energy that is created and spewed into the atmosphere can theoretically aid a spirit or entity in manifesting itself. This is one of those seldom used items popular when paranormal study was in its infancy. I am not going to go into detail here, but if this tool interests you, you may want to further study Kirlian photography which uses energy to theoretically capture auras. An aura is like a halo or a self generated radiation that surrounds even inanimate objects. Auras have been a staple of paranormal and psychic research for well over 100 years.

- **Thermal Imager**

 Some believe a thermal imager may be the very best piece of equipment for paranormal investigation, but unfortunately, it is the most expensive. Renowned for its uses in combat and law enforcement and even winterization, it has become the holy grail of paranormal gear. Contractors have used it to insulate houses, law enforcement has used it to find dropped evidence, marijuana groves and criminals while our military counts on it to isolate terrorists and weaponry. Thermal imaging permits you to actually view cold and heat. Cold appears in darker colors on the screen. The thermal imager allows you to save this information as different media in the form of images and with more expense, video. These abilities make the paranormal applications obvious.

There is no "quick fix" to acquiring thermal imaging. It is very expensive, and it is a luxury. There are different manufacturers, and none of them are in SaleMart. Although a Thermal Imager may theoretically, at last, get you the evidence that you actually have seen a spirit, there is a big negative. They may also simply show you an image from the previous teammate that has left a butt print on the sofa. In my opinion, instead of a Thermal Imager, buy a team van.

- **TriField Meter**

TriField EMF Meters detect electric field, magnetic fields, and microwave or radio fields. They are a visual gauge and although very accurate, they are not my first choice for onsite mobile investigation. I do like them for sit down contact work where some lighting is available and for running pre-hunt checks.

There are different settings on a TF EM meter for magnetic, electric, or radio/microwave. Magnetic may be the most useful during an investigation as it may indicate the existence of more than one field. As usual, activity is measured with our 1.5 rule for magnetic and microwave readings to 3 volts for electronic. Ranges on the differing settings are from about 5 feet for magnetic to 20 feet for microwave. Again as with all meters, locate the source of the reading and log it.

- **Wind Meter**

An Anemometer (Wind Meter) detects wind speed and

wind direction. Some believe that when a spirit manifests itself, a gust or breeze can be generated. The UPST has found the wind meter useful in other ways. Oftentimes, cold spots can influence an investigator and even his infrared thermometer. Wind meters allow your paranormal team to rule out ordinary causes for cold spots, such as drafts, furnace ductwork, etc. A wind meter is also very useful in outside locales. At one of our outside investigations, a temperature differential of nearly 15 degrees was detected at about 3 feet from the ground. The wind meter made it possible to locate the source of the cold spot. The wind meter can usually be more helpful in debunking than in confirming the paranormal, and in being so is a great addition to your tool box.

TRADITIONAL FAVORITES or Inexpensive Luxuries

- **Candle**

    A simple candle is one of the first wind meters. Many mediums still use candles in their séances. A wavering candle flame while extolling EVP can be not only mood enhancing, but exciting.

- **Extension cords and Electrical strips**

    Be sure to have adequate power supply for your investigation. Your pre-hunt will present you with all the electrical realities of your particular hunt. For instance, you may have loads of outlets and access to them by extension cord as in the Seul Choix Point Lighthouse or Riverside Cemetery, but none at all in the Helmer House Inn. If you don't have pre-charged back up batteries, move these items to the necessity list.

- **Flour or Talcum Powder**

    Hearing footsteps in the attic? A light dust of flour on the floor will let you know if it is physical. Only use this method in locations in which you have the ability to clean it up after your hunt.

- **Plastic Bags / Paper Bags / gloves / culture swabs**

    Plastic bags are used to protect evidence. The UPST has bagged many items including chess pieces, photos and even unusual hair discovered in a U.P. forest. Rich Meyers of the Rep. of the UPBFSO (U.P. Bigfoot Sasquatch Org.) recommended a paper bag to preserve DNA results (being tested at this printing). If you find something odd, out of place or extraordinary, put on some gloves and bag it. In addition, you may have a Doctor or nurse friend that can get you some "culture swab" tubes for smaller item collection. These are the tubes used to take samples of everything from saliva to moles for biopsy. If you find evidence on a hunt, ask the owner if you can take it for examination and if they'd like, return it after you're done.

- **Tool kit**

The UPST brings along many tools in a small kit. We recommend you bring an electric drill and several bits, screwdrivers, pliers, etc. If you are investigating an historical site, you may have to unscrew security barricades and it could be your responsibility. Come prepared.

We, at the UPST, always carry a battery diagnostic meter, a multi-tester, and <u>many</u> batteries. Electronic

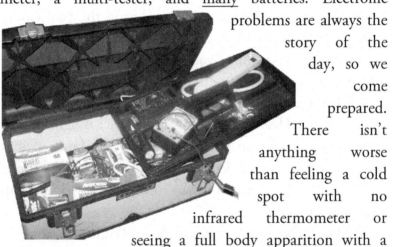

problems are always the story of the day, so we come prepared. There isn't anything worse than feeling a cold spot with no infrared thermometer or seeing a full body apparition with a dead battery in your video camera. Batteries are cheap, evidence costs hours and hours of work. Due diligence in all matters electronic will pay off in more ways than you can imagine.

Every day there is new equipment and tools being invented and used in paranormal investigation. It is impossible to itemize them all, but suffice it to say that you should keep an open mind regarding any new development. The UPST itself has invented several techniques and tools for paranormal investigation. Be creative when dealing with the unknown, nobody is an expert, and your imagination is the limit.

"Who's that?" A hushed voice came from the upstairs room.
"It's David and Christian," I said.

We quietly made our way up the stairway and peered into room 6. There was a heavy feeling in this area that was perceptible. Earlier in the evening Dave F. had captured some orbs on his digital camera and had informed me that he thought this was a hot spot.

"Something just touched me."
Betty lay on her side in the cold bedroom.
Christian and I stood quietly as Betty described physical interaction with the spirit we referred to as Uncle Gilbert.

"I was going though the regular EVP questions," Betty said.
"And I asked if he could touch me."
I could tell by the look in her eyes that this was no joke.
"Where at?" I asked.
Betty described two brushes on her cheek, both in response to her communication.

"Shouldn't we leave the camera?" Christian chimed in.

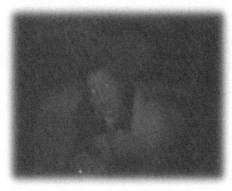

– Helmer House Inn – January 25, 2010, 11:45 pm

8

Organizing the Hunt

So you have formed your team, you have administered the PASS evaluation and have procured at least the basics in equipment. Time to get to the O.Z.!

Finding the Ghosts

Organization is the point where your researcher performs their most important function: setting locations and getting the history. The acquisition of sites is not just a one person job, but can be shared between all team members. For instance, if you are the leader of the team, you have obviously gained some ideas as to where you can and should investigate. Others on your team will have some suggestions as well. Discuss them with your team. Remember the old song "Anticipation?" Leaking a bit of information regarding potential hunts in advance only raises the interest and the excitement in the investigation.

Before you advance one of your team members to a research role, be careful to make sure that this person is ready for the job. Your future researcher is easily identified because she or he will be the team member that after hearing the next location calls you back with additional information. The researcher is never laidback and awaiting details, but is constantly studying for the next hunt.

At this point lets list a few of the prime locations where your Researcher or team can go to find potential locations for investigations.

- Books, magazines and newspapers – There are many good sources of information for haunted locations, and probably near where you live. This book, for instance, will give you a list of Michigan locations within its pages. Books on ghost towns of a region are always popular and have come in handy to us at the UPST.

- Historical Societies – These organizations collect an amazing menagerie of information about an area, all from one locale. We recommend joining one and making friends with the organizers. They are usually very well informed and nice people excited to share the history of their site and locations.

- Tourist Centers and Chambers of Commerce - Most communities have these types of centers which you can access through phone, email or in person. If you can't get information directly, usually these facilities can steer you in the right direction. Many cities actually have "ghost tours," which are like nighttime walking trips through local paranormal history, and an excellent training tool for young ghost hunters.

- Museums and Libraries - These offer local documentation and exhibits that explain the history and other interesting points of a spot or location. You will also find that a librarian or archivist is likely knowledgeable of the area, their facility, and willing to talk about possible hauntings in their region.

- Internet Options - The internet and the benefits to your team will be explored more in an upcoming chapter but let me summarize for purposes of this list and organizing your hunt. The internet offers access to birth and death records, cemeteries, and regional history. Perhaps one of the most satisfying aspects of the internet are the "friend making" tools that will help you network with other paranormal teams like yourself for exchange of information. You will want to address the next chapter for a better understanding of internet use.

- Grandpa and Grandma – Some of our best resources live up the road in the form of grandparents or seniors. These valued citizens are walking encyclopedias of local knowledge and stories, and tapping into this extensive knowledge is usually as easy as asking. Be polite, and have the time to listen. You will not regret it.

Just a note on contact when doing research for your hunt: Introduce yourself and explain what you do. You may want to add that this is "the way we teach our children and team to respect our local history." Your short opening should allow your source to take over the conversation. If they have questions about your team, they will ask. Remember that you are there to listen and to learn. Be polite but inquisitive and you will discover that most people love to share their knowledge.

Team, Time and Date

The next part of the O.Z. (organizing), after you have put together your team roster and picked a location for

the investigation, is to set the team, time and date. A team roster is a list of hunters that you have assembled from which you may have to pick a select team depending on the size of the location. Many UPST investigations are offered on a first come, first serve basis.

Most outside locations are "the more the merrier," and can be the very best training sites. You may have to make cuts for inside locations which I recommend you do on a combination of seniority and reliability combined with "first come, first serve." As I discussed earlier in the forming the team chapter, you will run into those that already scratched their itch and will no longer have the interest. Always attempt to leave room for the impassioned newbie, but be sure to have an experienced team member for them to partner with initially. For small indoor locations limit your team to 2 or 3 person groups per area of the house. Of course, there are exceptions; the House of Ludington is extensive. Does that mean we go in with a team of twenty?

No. Even with multiple floors and a huge expanse, a large team runs on top of each other. You don't need extra thumps and noises coming from two floors above. What happens if you accidentally oversize the group on an investigation? You can enlarge the groups up to four or five members or, if the location is extremely limited in size, you can arrange to walk in shifts with one team doing outside investigation or simply waiting in a vehicle. Be sure to be fair with the time allotted each group. I always make a Time Grid that shows me where each group is and I then rotate them (swing them) every 45 minutes. This is unless activity is being detected by a team, where I will then allow them a double shift. The easiest thing to do is never go into any location without putting a realistic number to the team.

Time and date must be arranged around your team, the proprietors of the location and weather conditions if it is an outside hunt. Arranging investigations around your team can be tricky, and in the end you will have to nail down a date with the owner actually becoming the master of you and your team's destiny. We have had many investigations that have gone ahead without members of our team based on their very busy schedule. In all honestly, it hasn't impacted any investigation in the least. If you have a full roster there are plenty of replacements. Remember: don't work too hard to get someone to have fun. As far as a particular time, after dark is always best for many reasons like ambience, excitement, silence, etc. Some theorize that spirits are more active at night. Some believe there is more inert energy for them to draw on for manifestation. And of course, it is quieter aiding EVP collection. It doesn't hurt that nightfall is after work either. Again, the time is based on the convenience of the owner or manager of the location.

Transit and Travel

Ok, now your O.Z. has progressed to the travel stage. If the hunt is local, meeting at the house is alright if you have room to park. Some locales have a parking lot nearby. It is always better to travel as a team with multiple members in a car because this allows for more preparation that you don't have to cover at the location. We also converse with our two-ways or cell phones on the way to the site. Remember to make sure if you are sharing a ride that no one has to leave an investigation early; this is taboo to any quality team. Covering expenses can be done in many ways. Usually the UPST splits gasoline and lodging cost if necessary. Other teams opt for a membership and dues structure to support their hunts, but we find that this plan can dissuade potential members. We believe that if you want to incorporate a dues system, do it after you have created the necessary commitment to maintain your core team along with extra costs attributed equally to the non-regulars. Otherwise, split the extra costs between your team.

Team UPST unloads at Fayette

On Site for the Hunt

Now you are at the hunt, so what do you do? By now your team leader should have the equipment and team assignments recorded on your equipment log sheets. Your tech manager will distribute the equipment, or if your team members carry their own, your tech manager may upgrade them. Everyone should have at least a flashlight, but let your tech manager handle this. I usually schedule the equipment dispersal during or just before the walk through.

On the walk through, always carry a camera. The UPST experiences phenomena during pre-hunt walks on a surprisingly regular basis. Moving objects and sometimes even an occasional EVP can be recorded on the first time around. Usually the owner will take you on a tour of the premises and then you as leader will pass this on to the team. Some leaders opt to take their tech manager with them, but the UPST usually uses the researcher and allows this time for the Q to do his duty distributing the equipment. Later on, the team leader and the Tech will discuss basic equipment locations and static cameras.

The Investigation

So, the equipment has been handed out and it is time to start the fun! First, the lead will take the rest of the team on their walk through. He will give a pointed

summary of what the proprietor presented along with an increased focus on further technical aspects and coming group responsibilities. After the team leader takes the

team on its walk through, he will specifically designate the groups and locations, make sure they have their log forms, pens and begin the hunt. When the teams are prepared to go, our lights out signal is "Dead time! Spook On." Many hours will pass before "Spook Off," is heard. After a pre-set time (again depending upon activity) the leader will switch locations and line-ups if necessary. If something is happening at a particular location making it detrimental to leave, the group will radio the lead and inform him so he can work around them. In other words, if you are having an EVP conversation with a long dead president, inform the team leader that you are going to "hang" for awhile. After your sweep, log all information even if little happens and be sure to allow your squad a few minutes between swings. It will greatly aid during the post-hunt analysis.

Take only Pictures, leave only Ectoplasm

Unfortunately, it's "Spook Off" or time to wrap. Everyone will finish out their final logs as your techie inventories in the equipment. Always do a final sweep through the site checking for errant equipment and making sure that there are no signs of your team having been there. "Take only pictures and leave only ectoplasm," in fact, don't even leave ectoplasm if possible! While on the way home is a great time to go over details with your team, so don't put away the two-ways or cells until the last moment. You will be pleased with the information that surfaces when the memories are still fresh. Have someone (preferably your researcher) record or take notes. So, you finally arrive at your homes, everyone has their equipment and a good time was had by all. Another investigation is in the books, right? WRONG!

ANALYSIS - Time for the GEEK Squad

Now the analysis begins. We count on the computer tech or GEEK to download the info from the recording devices and hopefully burn this media to CD or post it on our website for dispersion to your team. It is difficult if not impossible handling this important function alone. As your team progresses and individuals invest in their own equipment, this step will become easier for your geek. The UPST owns several night vision pieces and recorders so this process can still offer hours and hours of information to review. In one overnight investigation I and our tech manager had over 64 hours of infrared video to analyze and this didn't include the audio mp3 recordings or the photographs. When selling this tedious job to your geek, techie or other, make sure that they realize that they will be the first to actually view any evidence you may have collected. Be sure as team leader to publicly recognize their commitment and or any other discovery they make. I will tell you a simple ploy the UPST created to work through this analysis more quickly later in the Onboard for Online chapter. The other information from the rest of the team, whether distributed by the geek, or collected on their own equipment should come back to you carefully logged with time signature. For instance, Joe Leduc, one of our UPST investigators once submitted an MP3 from an investigation where he had meticulously logged when and where he discovered any anomaly for my second hear verification. This makes it much easier to review hours of evidence. Have your analysts listen and view with a pencil ready to take notes that will reflect location, group and time.

After the evidence has been compiled, it is the geek's additional job to upload the recorded evidence for posting online at the team site or on a video distribution site (like YouTube) for the rest of the team's viewing and analysis. The sharing of this information simply creates interest. You will find that your team watches the hunt video rather than reality television like American Idiot.

Chapter 8
The Real Wrap & Reveal

After the analysis, the leader should vigilantly assemble all the information into logs, edited video and audio format for examination by the owner, manager or proprietor of the hunt site. It is always a pleasure to reveal evidence attained by your team to the principles of a location. It speaks to your team's professionalism and usually consolidates the feelings and views of the owner. If nothing is discovered, as the representative of your team, you should still make a full report to the owner. Don't worry when the worst scene scenario will only be that "we didn't catch it this time, call us and we'll come back."

Perception

As a paranormal team, you are in the field of human services. You want to maintain a reputation that is beyond reproach. This means that the team will demonstrate an understanding and professionalism that supersedes outward

displays of ignorance in the presence of the homeowner, proprietor, etc. In other words, save questions for the team until after you are alone as a team. If someone asks to pay for your team services we, at the UPST, recommend you not accept money. There are teams that look for more than to break even and due to infrequent investigations, conferences have become their business. This is very sad.

We have accepted overnights and meals in the past, but we always treat the homeowner with the respect given someone who has offered us a great favor or gift. The wonderful thing about this field is that if you O.Z. the hunt professionally and respectfully, the owner will understand that you have also done them a service and invite you back. Occasionally, you will be asked to pay for your stay and investigation. Usually this means that the chances of this particular hotel, restaurant or site using the paranormal as a marketing tool is very high and the opportunity that you have a significant investigation are slim to none. Opt instead for a site that wants you to document their activity for them at no cost! If this is a mutually beneficial situation, than there should be no charge either way. If the facility believes they are doing you a favor, chances are they know you won't discover evidence that they can use to promote their business. The advertising that a team supplies any site is far beyond a room fee and the owners that realize this offer a real hunt with real action!

In rare cases, compensation for your team may be in order, but this is the fodder for another book on professional investigation to be addressed in the future. It is our job here to get you hunting. On an aside, in my many years of paranormal investigating experience (since 1974), I have run into many paranormal squads and have only met one professional team worth the money that they asked for and many amateur teams that should have been paid. Being professional in the paranormal game has very little to do with making money. Cancellations, punctuality, professionalism and follow-up will track your team through its existence. I must tell you a story that came from a bar/restaurant that has allowed paranormal investigation in the past. It seems that a team from a college town in the Upper Peninsula of Michigan was allowed in to investigate. The owner waited past their arrival time for an hour and a half and finally closed. The team called a week later and stated that a close personal friend had been involved in an auto accident and apologized profusely. The owner rescheduled with them. This time they were over 45 minutes late and apologized again. The owner gave them the walk through and left returning the next morning to find the door unlocked and that they'd left a cooler with beer in it. He never heard from them again. Six months later a team under a different name arranged an investigation. When the owner met them he was shocked to see that this was nearly the same team that had treated his business so disrespectfully just a few months earlier. He asked them to leave.

Not every location is the Paulding Light. Even though the UPST has gained great respect from the State of Michigan and the rangers at Paulding, we still do all that is necessary to maintain the good will of the owners and authorities that monitor different locations.

Christian's B'day at Paulding with cake from Betty!

Yes, it is true that we always offer law enforcement hotdogs and cake! They like us and we like them. I will go into the Paulding Light and other outside practice more in the *UPST Case Study Digest.* I will also tell the story of a funny hoaxster that I couldn't help but give a hotdog.

Always remember, that as your team forges ahead, concentrate on building elevated aspirations and reputation. The O.Z. (OrganiZation) is what your team reputation will be based on when it is judged by outside observers. A quality team has no need to change its name.

"No way am I friggin' going in there." Zippo stated snippily.

Bongo and Rylie had opted for the van rather than this cold and creepy building, but Zippo and Bryson stood at the door. Flashlight beams swept the interior of the dilapidated farm house as its history spun around the room. This old monstrosity was the origin of a local ghost story that had been passed down for nearly 60 years. The legend is that as a motorist travels by, an eerie light can be seen inside the abandoned building; strange phenomena or spirit?

"What do you see?" Bryson asked.
Christian and I stood on the intact part of the floor and breathed in the chill air.
"Not much more than you do" I answered as I explored the back room. *"Go ahead son."*
I directed Christian to start the EVP work which he had grown accustomed to.
*"Mr. D***********, do you feel bad that your house is wrecked?"*
As Christian spoke, I felt a chill run from the top of my head to the floor.
Christian whispered, "There's something here."

– The D*********** Estate – 10:15 pm

9

Onboard for Online

The last few years have seen an amazing change in how we O.Z. our paranormal investigations. Much of the research and communication once necessary to obtain through leg work, telephone calls or snail mail, can now be acquired in your own home. Computers and the internet have not only impacted every facet of modern life, this technology has profoundly changed the science of paranormal investigation. It took me a while to jump into the 90's, but after I did, I found out what the internet had to offer the UPST. What I plan to discuss in this chapter is broken down into the following sections:

- Online Research
- Online Investigation Frosting
- Online Post Investigation Research and Posting

Online Research

We have already discussed some of the responsibilities of the team researcher, and thank the lord for the internet! The UPST's researchers Betty Lustila and Brenda Raymond recommend "due diligence" in accessing the great abundance of information on the net. Personal details of death, birth, place of internment and much more can be explored with a little patience, but sometimes that information is not found overnight. Don't limit yourself and keep the sites in your favorites for multi-accessing searches. What we would like to do here now is present you with a few websites that will get you started on the research for your next hunt.

- Genealogy Today has been publishing unique information and offering innovative services since 1999. Their goal is to help everyone that visits and hope to become one of your favorite providers of history, genealogy and family history resources. www.genealogyToday.com
- Ancestor Search has been helping those interested in researching their family history find genealogy databases since 1997! The Ancestor Search genealogy portal can find most family history & surname origin for personal or investigation research. www.searchforancestors.com
- FamilySearch is the largest genealogy organization in the world. Millions of people use FamilySearch

records, resources, and services to learn more about their family history. For over 100 years, FamilySearch has been actively gathering, preserving, and sharing genealogical records worldwide. Patrons may freely access their resources and service online at FamilySearch.org, or through over 4,500 family history centers in 70 countries, including the renowned Family History Library in Salt Lake City, Utah. Very useful for paranormal pre-hunt research. www.familysearch.org

- Ancestor Hunt. Search for ancestors and locate family surnames in some of the best and largest free genealogy databases online. Start with the Genealogy Search Engines and Contents menu found on each page so you won't get lost. Then browse the free genealogy resources found on the matching page. www.ancestorhunt.com

- Historic Maps Restored. This organization started with a map library of nearly 300 maps, all of which were originals with a good portion of them within the state of California. But when demand grew, it didn't take them long to realize they were going to need a wider variety of maps. We have used these on many ghost town and outdoor hunts. The restored map library consists of about 1650 historical maps dating back to the sixteenth century. The archives hold another 6-7000 maps awaiting restoration. www.historicmapsrestored.com

- Interment Net. A free online library of cemetery records from thousands of cemeteries across the world, for historical and genealogy research www.interment.net

- Find a Grave. Like Interment, Find a grave offers thousands of cemeteries and graves nationwide. Although the staff that mans this site is overall short sighted and dim, the contributor base is great. www.findagrave.com

- Grave Locator. Search for burial locations of veterans and their family members in VA National Cemeteries, state veterans cemeteries, various other military and Department of Interior cemeteries, and for veterans buried in private cemeteries when the grave is marked with a government grave marker. This Nationwide Gravesite Locator includes burial records from many sources. These sources provide varied data; some searches may contain less information than others. Information on veterans buried in private cemeteries was collected for furnishing government grave markers, but there is no information available for burials prior to 1997. www.gravelocator.cem.va.gov/j2ee/servlet/NGL_v1

- Michigan Department of Education eLibrary, Genealogy Gateway. Whether you are charting your family tree, researching your ancestry or seeking information on family or social history, the resources you'll find in this gateway will get you started or move you forward in your research quest. . www.mel.org/SPT--BrowseResourcesGenealogy.php?ParentId=839

- Use YouTube, PhotoBucket and other free posting sites to share the results of your hunt.

www.youtube.com

www.photobucket.com

- And don't forget the Upper Peninsula Spook Team's home page. There are over 500 hours of video, audio, links, comments and digital photos posted here.

www.upspookteam.info

Of course a good old Google or Bing search will often aid you in tracking down that elusive bit of info that gives a  direction to the hunt. Be creative in your search technique and try different tacts. For example, you might search: "Mackinac county cemetery list." Let me give you a more in depth avenue we took on one hunt. We had a young man that had supposedly committed suicide at a residence. Our online search started with his name, town and the word obituary. It then moved to the name of the "local paper," the word "obituary" and to the year "1978." Every bit of info you find will further aid you in finding new search words and often will spawn more pertinent and usable information for the hunt.

Online Investigation Frosting

The internet can be integral to almost all aspects of the hunt and not limited to just research. The UPST uses online services such as Skype for pre and post hunt information sharing and communication. For instance, we have had up to 22 members taking part in a pre-hunt prep and this service is absolutely free. It allows the freedom of allowing questions and answers and outright communication between all members. Always maintain polite listening skills and address the leader to speak if you have a question or something important to offer. Whoever is speaking at the time should be addressed before offering further information. This cuts down on cross-talk issues. Other programs such as Google talk can be used, but we have had good luck with Skype.

Another use for online communication occurs when on a hunt. You can actually bring other team members, psychics or just observers to the investigation. If the location you are investigating has wifi, you can carry around your colleague on laptop or tablet through Skype and they will have total audio/visual access to your hunt. The UPST has used this technique many times in the past to include absent members and even psychics. Believe it or not many pieces of evidence have been gained through the use of our psychic member from the west coast. Although she has flown to the Midwest to join the UPST on many occasions, she is primarily with us via Skype video/audio.

In addition, I have actually conducted UPST academies through Skype which allows you video as well as audio. No matter your format, this "face time" is valuable in setting up investigations as well as the inevitable debriefing.

www.skype.com

Online Post Investigation Research and Posting

I've already mentioned how pre and post hunt conversation can be pursued through Skype online but now we are going to take it to the next level. The UPST created a website many years ago for the exclusive function of sharing evidence. What we do is post unedited video, audio and photos so that the whole team can analyze the information. If not the first, we are one of the first teams that offered this evidence sharing technique and it has played out quite nicely. In the old days, the media would be submitted to "me" to go through... now with the advent of the internet, EVERYONE gets to share the pain. I, of course, say that jokingly because we have members of the UPST that relish the analysis! I have to point out

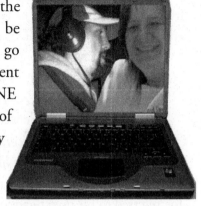

Robert Declercq and Linda Caron who both have an amazing ability to stay focused on media. They've turned in evidence I had overlooked and occasionally, I stick a bounty on first and best evidence, history, etc. Linda has won before. Research medals have in the past also fallen to Jason (Zoop) Zupancic and Melissa Olson who always seem to find information that is interesting and obscure.

But I digress; the purpose of this section is to point out how the UPST shares the chore of sifting through all evidence. This practice not only makes it easier for me but offers new eyes and ears to the process; many times more accurate and more open minded. As I said, we currently have over 500 hours of media at www.upspookteam.info and although much of it is private (team only due to client confidentiality), all of the public academies and conferences are public. Check it out and come connect with us at a future UPST academy to join the team.

"Did you guys hear that?

Bryson breathed heavily as he crossed the cemetery to meet Joe Leduc, Christian and myself. We all stood listening to a ringing that sounded similar to a cowbell in the foggy distance.

"Yeah," I whispered.

"We heard it, seems like it came from out by the gate."

There was a long silence and the bell rang again.

"Are you recording this Joe?"

"Yeah," Joe continued. "I've had it on… and I think Bryson and I recorded the sounds of the children laughing."

Joe referred to his investigation along with Bryson in what is locally referred to as the "Kids Cemetery." A plot isolated in this same graveyard that hid multitudes of children that died during the 1918 influenza epidemic.

Cell Phone recording from Joe Leduc one week later:

"David, you'll never guess what I have on my MP3 recorder!"

– The Lakeview Cemetery, Manistique, MI 11:17 pm

122

10

Seul Choix Pointe Lighthouse
Case Study I

It was January 31st, and the snow swirled amongst the three foot drifts that surrounded the proclaimed "Most haunted lighthouse on the Great Lakes." Over 150 documented incidences seemed to confirm this assertion. Team UPST, along with Marilyn Fisher, the president of the Gulliver Historical Society, broke trail through the snow while dragging our equipment toward the rear entrance of the keeper's quarters. Bringing in our gear was no easy task. Thank God for young bucks like Joseph and Bryson as Christian is too young, and I am, hmmm, let us say… in a position of authority…LOL. After much struggle all was inside and although the facility is closed for the season, they leave the heat on: BONUS. As you know by now, I am David Lawrence, the leader of the Upper Peninsula Spook Team. I had named a skeleton crew of nephew Bryson Lawrence, Joe Leduc and then seven year old son Christian; experienced investigators all. Marilyn Fischer led our team inside and the unpacking began.

The Seul Choix Pointe Lighthouse was actually commissioned in 1886 with a congressional appropriation to protect ships from the Upper Peninsula's craggy southern shore. But between negotiations with the owner of the land and the potential contractors, the building didn't start until 1892. A temporary fourth order light was installed in that same year and ran until the structure was finished in 1895. For over 120 years, at first the Fresnel lens (a superior French made lamp) and now an airport beacon have shot a beam of light into the mist and the weather aiding the brave mariners of Lake Michigan. Seul Choix was purchased from the Coast Guard in 1977 by the Michigan Department of Natural Resources, but has been managed and restored by the Gulliver Historical Society since 1987. The exterior gables were constructed in the manner of a boat bow bent ever so beautifully in reverence to the shape of the typical wooden schooner that graced Lake Michigan when the lighthouse was built. All of the grounds are meticulously kept up and the keeper's quarters seemed to welcome our team. Upon walking into this historical site, we are taken with the absolute integrity in which the structure had been maintained. It is beautiful within as well as out. Inside we experienced a very uplifting setting room indicative of the early 1900's. Seul Choix has become one of the ultimate tourist destinations in the state of Michigan. Tonight, it is a ghost hunting destination for the Upper Peninsula Spook Team. *CN: I like Seul Choix because it feels like home... like someone still lives there.*

Although, I had been here before and conducted EVP sessions for years with my son, I had never had the opportunity to investigate the lighthouse in a full overnight investigation. As I said, Christian and I have visited Seul Choix Pointe many times over the years making many new friends. We have come to know regular staff volunteers, such as Bob and Naomi Sanders, Bob Williams (the Captain Townshend re-enactor), and seasonal caretakers Julie and Rory. Of course at the moment, renowned Historian Marilyn Fischer led us through the structure. Marilyn related at least a dozen tales that she and others had experienced here at haunted Seul Choix. Stories transpired of moving chairs, silverware, bible pages, the odor of cigar smoke and even multiple sightings of a full body apparition that is evidently Captain Joseph "Willy" Townshend.

Walking into the dining room, we were all pleasantly surprised to see a fork flipped upside down on a plate in typical British fashion. The house has been locked since Christmas and everything left in its proper place, so this seemed to indicate activity in the last six weeks. Marilyn told us that the fork upside down is definitely a clue pointing to the Captain and his British heritage. We photographed the table and the fork before replacing the instrument in its proper place. Leaving the dining room, we were now listening intently to Marilyn in the kitchen when suddenly:

"Hey! The bible page is different." Bryson exclaimed excitedly from the previous room.

Marilyn, Christian, Joe and I all walked quickly back to the dining room where Bryson had straggled. He stood with a quizzical look on his face panning between me and the open bible.

"Are you sure?" I asked skeptically.

"Oh yeah… it had a picture on it before."

We had only been in the kitchen for about five minutes so the page would have had to turn while we were there. I asked Bryson to find the page that he had seen earlier upon entering the house and he did so, three to the right of the now open page. We turned the bible to its original position and I went about trying to debunk the occurrence. I walked past at different angles and at different paces, attempting to create the breeze needed to move the pages. I had our group try to duplicate it in the order and position that  we had originally walked. We couldn't get even one page to stir. Things were already getting interesting. We returned to the kitchen where Marilyn told us more Seul Choix history, including the fact that the only original piece of furniture in the house was the table in front of us now. It had been found in pieces in the basement and reassembled. At this table there is one chair that purportedly moves on its own. We listened to several stories about it, one taking place in this room experienced by a State Police officer (hardly a nervous or gullible fellow) and yet another having been documented on tape by a nationally televised paranormal program. Marilyn swung the conversation back to the most famous of Seul Choix's ghostly inhabitants: Captain Joseph "Willy" Townshend.

Townshend was originally from Bristol, England and after his stint as a Captain moved to Canada where he was offered the job as the second head lighthouse keeper of Seul Choix. Captain Townshend was a rigid man, very uniform in his duties and what he believed the responsibilities of a lighthouse keeper were. He performed these tasks with precision and attention to detail which had a tendency to irritate his assistant lighthouse keepers. This didn't bother Captain Townshend. He had the experience and the knowledge to ward off the threats that faced his sea bound brethren and he was ironclad obliged to keep them from coming to ill fate on Seul Choix point. The Captain was the lighthouse keeper from 1901 until 1910. He died a painful death most likely from cancer, was embalmed in the basement and then laid out for visitation in the first floor parlor for several days. The vat (sink) that Townshend was drained into during the funeral process remains in the basement of the building. It also seems that the Captain remains; smoking his cigars and walking the long winding steps of the lighthouse. The actual light tower is 78 feet, 9 inches and is accessed with a circular wrought iron staircase that winds clockwise to the top level. Captain Townshend traversed this route several times a day observing weather, making sure the oil was ample and the Fresnel lamp spotless. This schedule continued through the night when the keeper was responsible for making sure the lamp had oil and good wicks as it burnt. If there is such a thing as a paranormal magnet, Seul Choix Pointe lighthouse may just be it. Picture a structure built on limestone (rock) and nearly surrounded by Lake Michigan. Since the beginning of written time, there have been legends that whisper of a spirit's inability to cross open water. Combine this with a rocky peninsula, an iron staircase that twirls up to the top of the light and you have the makings of what may be a paranormal lightening rod or antenna.

Marilyn continued her Seul Choix Pointe Lighthouse lessons as our team followed her from room to room and ghost story to ghost story. Another surprise met us in the Seul Choix room. As Joe, Bryson and Marilyn stood with me at the entrance to the parlor, I heard Christian call to me from up the hall.

"Hey Daddy, come and see this."

We entered the Seul Choix display room. Christian

pointed out a very large and heavy lighthouse replica approximately two and ½ feet tall that appeared to have been pushed off of its display table. It leaned precariously balanced against the wall. Marilyn was flabbergasted.

"This would never have been left like this on closing," she said.

"And it's too heavy to move itself," Bryson added. *CN: It was a big model; I think it was too big to have been moved by accident.*

We again documented this possible kinetic activity on digital camera as Marilyn continued to extol history. The name Seul Choix is French for "last choice" and is popularly pronounced "Sis-Shwa." The early French voyageurs recognized the importance of Seul Choix Pointe as a safe haven in times of rough weather on the majestic, yet dangerous Lake Michigan. There was no better place to put a lighthouse and even then, some say as many as 250 sailors lost their lives just off Seul Choix Pointe. This, in addition to the early occupation by Native Americans, led to rich legend such as Rock Spirits said to have been seen by early fisherman as they put in at dusk on the Pointe. In fact, some contend that when the white man developed Seul Choix as a fishing community, they actually dug up an Indian burial ground, engaging in horse play with the skulls as they constructed the road to the water. In another odd piece of history, fisherman Isaac Blanchard was killed by Augustus Pond, on June 18[th,] 1859, inside the grounds of the old Seul Choix fishing village. It seems Blanchard was one of three men harassing Augustus Pond continually for days when the victim finally borrowed a double barrel shotgun out of fear for his family and his own life. He ended up shooting Blanchard, even though it seems that Dave Plant was actually the instigator of the trio. Pond was convicted of manslaughter though making the argument of self defense. This led to an appeal and a reversal of the decision that set forth the principle of self defense still applied nationwide in our courts today. Events such as these are abundant at Seul Choix Pointe and also contribute to the haunted history of this otherwise serene and scenic spot. The combination of the natural attributes of this paranormal magnet, along with the Native American lore and the death of the many sailors and fishermen has led to the perfect paranormal storm. Many believe that the mundane duties of a lighthouse keeper performed repeatedly over many years in this environment have led to the sound of footsteps and other residual spirit activity being locked in the fabric of time.

"What is that?" Christian pointed near Marilyn's foot just inside the doorway entrance of the Captain's room. Halting her narrative for a moment, she leaned over, picked up the small piece of paper and looked at it. With a bemused, yet knowing look she handed me what appeared to be a small name tag and on it was one word: Christian.

As I alluded to earlier, the UPST has visited Seul Choix many times in the past and Christian performed some of his earliest EVP work here at the age of five. His childlike questions like "what is your favorite color?" have become staples of the UPST EVP dialogue. In fact, since the early video was posted on our website, I hear this same question being asked by every team on television. I digress, anyway, back to the tag. Christian and I had visited 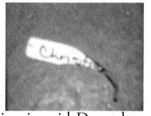 Seul Choix for its Christmas celebration in mid December. It seems that all the children at the celebration received a name tag. Later I would refer to the guest register to discover forty-three parents and their children had registered that day. All of these children with tags, and one bearing my son's name is found inside the normally gated room of Captain Townshend? Only later after talking with Marilyn, I discovered that ninety-six different children had received gifts on that day and some people had not signed in for their kids. It was as though the Captain was letting Christian know he was welcome. It was quite a coincidence I thought, but after what has already happened today, I wondered if it weren't more.

Marilyn Fischer said her farewells, wished us luck and fought her way back through the snow as we finished unpacking our equipment trunks. It was about 3:30 in the afternoon and we had just enough time to unload, set up, take a quick daylight walkthrough, charge our batteries and eat before it got dark. Nightfall comes early in the Upper Peninsula and even after the fall time change, 5:30 or 6 is about as late as the sun shines. Our tasks were accomplished quickly as we didn't want to waste an extra minute in beginning the investigation.

The equipment we brought for this hunt included 5 infrared cameras, one with each team after we split, and 2 set up to run statically at points of interest in the house. These locations include Captain Townshend's room and the dining room where the bible pages had turned. The last camera was saved for back up as it was a mini-dv and used tape. Mp3 recorders would be set up in the lighthouse tower as well as in the parlor. Carry along equipment included EMF detectors, an infrared thermometer, 2 digital cameras, and of course, flashlights. Joe Leduc opts to wear a head lamp in most cases and since I have always recommend keeping the lights off unless you absolutely need them, Joe's lamp is the only light on in the later investigation and allowed only his red lamps to keep the level low. In addition, we will employ UPST ghost traps.

The first ghost trap is "crosshair" design and is positioned with a fresh British Corona on the main stairwell banister as I discussed earlier in chapters on equipment. The cigar is what we call a "chrono-trigger." It is an item,

sound, smell, etc. that appeals to the time period or targeted spirit. The second "bulls-eye" ghost trap is placed in the Captain's and Lenore's bedroom on the floor with a marble that when employing EVP, we will ask them to move. Photos are again taken of the item's beginning positions to compare with those taken at the end of the hunt.

After a quick ham sandwich and some Dill Pickle Potato Chips (a U.P. & Minnesota delicacy), we did our daytime pre-hunt walk through, photographing all furniture and especially the items that have been known to move in the past. I grabbed an infrared camera and Christian carried his EMF detector. We had already seen the keeper's quarters during Marilyn's tour but it was far more expansive than I had remembered. The lighthouse keeper's quarters is a two story building with a basement and an attic connected to the actual lighthouse tower. There are three bedrooms upstairs with a smaller room that has been converted into a bathroom. There are also a few closets on this level, one of which opens into the main hallway near the Captain's and Lenore Goudreau's bedrooms. William Blanchard, Townshend's assistant, took over after the death of the Captain and William Goudreau (Lenore's husband) later became Seul Choix's fourth lighthouse keeper. Lenore's ghost is also thought to linger here. Marilyn told us of the mirror in the bedroom that has been documented by a PBS television crew with a face in it. I had previously seen this video and I must admit it is rather startling.

On the first floor there is a parlor at the base of the two direction staircase which adjoins the dining room and through a hallway, the kitchen. There are two closets in this hallway. Also adjacent to the parlor is the pantry which leads to the back section of the first floor and the lighthouse entry. Down this short hallway are three rooms now set up as a second parlor, study or small music room indicative of the turn of the 19th century (it may have been a small bedroom at one time). There are two larger adjacent rooms, the first contains antiques indicative of maritime history. There is everything from old photographs to a Fresnel lens to antique diving equipment. The other room has a collection of special Seul Choix models and artistic renderings of the famous lighthouse. This is where we earlier found the overturned lighthouse replica. We reversed our course back to the main entry parlor, past this room behind a door, there is a small alcove which appears to be the spot where the keeper kept his records, and beyond that the door to the tower. We walked up the countless steps to the top of the lighthouse. Although the airport beacon spun around with a loud whir, the light had not yet engaged. The miles long view from the circular windows is breath taking. A pine covered Pointe gives way to a rocky shoreline lapped by the miles of pristine freshwater that is Lake Michigan. I realized quickly that there is too much noise at the top of the tower to leave an Mp3 recorder; we will leave it at the base of the steps.

"Ok, guys," I spoke as I moved toward the square hatch leading below, "Let's get downstairs and set an Mp3 recorder underneath the bottom step."

Heading down the circular spider web I noted how much easier it seemed than the long trek we had made just twenty minutes earlier. I had an admiration for Captain Townshend's devotion to a job that must have been repetitive and routine. As for the basement, it is accessed by a stairway off of the pantry. It is a maze of rooms that I have searched my way through many times in the effort to find the sink where Captain Townshend was embalmed, and I can still get turned around.

Bryson, Christian and I loaded the mini-dv recorder and checked the batteries in the hard drive infrareds and remaining equipment. Joe was sent to unscrew all the bulbs in the lighthouse as they remain on through the night. And yes, some were bulbs. This was, of course, before congress told us we had to switch to fluorescents in an effort to save the planet from global warming. Looking back at the years since this investigation, as it gets cooler and cooler in the winters I could use some global warming. On this night however, just staying warm in the tower was my bigger concern. Joe returned.

Joe running baseline EMF and getting ready to go dark

"I got em' all out David."

"Load up men we're hitting it," I said as I hung a second mini-flashlight around Christian's neck.

We stayed together for the first run through turning off the lights, setting the ghost traps and going dark through the complete structure. We had already erected the dining room and the upstairs bedroom infrareds. The hunt began.

***

Darkness had fallen. We'd set up headquarters in the pantry, and through the window, the sweeping light from the now engaged airport beacon could be seen illuminating the white of the snow outside. We decided to attack the tower! My team didn't know this at the time, but I was having blood pressure problems and this climb was extremely trying for me. In the video my huffing and puffing is clearly audible. I recommend you have a physical before you take on haunted locations like Seul Choix, Trans Allegheny Lunatic Asylum, the House of Ludington or the Shelton Hotel at Fayette. Going up and down stairs until dawn can be a test.

The light was nearly blinding as we completed our ascent to the heart of this beautiful structure. It was almost surreal looking at the power of the light as it shot a warning beam across the great expanse of Lake Michigan. It is said that the original oil powered Fresnel lens was at least equal to that of the current brightness, but standing in that tower I can only imagine.

"Hey, look there," I said. "I can see Inland from here."

"I think Inland is this way Uncle David," Bryson responded pointing directly opposite. Inland Quarry is a staple business in the local area and looks like a small city from the lighthouse. The realization came upon me that I'd clearly become  disoriented and Bryson was right. The light from the quarry was so strong that the reflection on the plate glass windows had given me an illusion of Inland's direction.

"Wow, you're right Brys, come over here and see what I am seeing."

The three of them moved behind me to see what I had seen, and this is when it happened. Whenever I am asked what my scariest moment on a ghost hunt was, this is the first thing that comes to mind.

"BANG, CLANG, Bang, bang, bang, crash, thud!" Christian had fallen through the open hatch down the very steep steps to the level below. The sound of the crashing EMF detector echoed as it hit the concrete and slid across the floor.

"Oh my God," I whispered… and held my breath; nothing but silence. Then:

"Dad! I think I broke my EMF detector!"

"…Don't worry about it, are you alright?"

"It's my EMF detector!" Christian was clearly more concerned about his tool than his health.

"Thank God," I thought as a sweet relief swept over me. Christian slowly came up the stairs and through the hatch holding what had been his EMF detector in three parts.

"Let me see it," I said now feeling a combination of fear, relief and anger. I took the tool from him and snapped it quickly back together…I turned it on and it lit up.

"Whew," Christian said through a sigh of relief.

"WHEW IS RIGHT! Watch what you're doing," I said firmly. "This hunt could have ended very quickly and very badly."

The only one of us that wasn't shaken by this incident appeared to be Christian, who immediately moved back across the platform to look at the lights of the Inland

Quarry. A vision of broken arms and legs or worse soon left my mind and we were back on the hunt.

CN: I was able to use my arms and my butt to slide down the steps to the next floor. I dropped my EMF detector and was more worried about that than my fall.

***

In the parlor now we are getting very hot readings on the EMF detector. Having already done our base readings on the walk through we found no readable electro magnetic fields, but now, at 7 to 7 ½ the tool squealed one long beep. After a minute or two the signal would subside and then as we conducted EVP the meter would again erupt with noise and light. For about ten minutes it was in and out and then all went quiet again. I decided we would enter the dining room and kitchen areas and check things out. The bible had not again changed its pages but suddenly from the kitchen came a yell of excitement.

"Uncle David! The chair moved."

Bryson stood next to Joe about three feet from the table. They were frozen as the awesomeness of what they saw washed over them. The chair that has been documented moving on such television shows as *Scariest Places on Earth* had not let us down. Having been firmly placed  under the table in our walk through, the chair had moved nearly 18 inches back and had spun to the left. This was more than enough that I could have sat down on it. The hunt was getting hot quickly.

"That's what I'm talking about!" I stated excitedly. I deemed this the perfect time to break into two teams to conduct EVP in different areas of the house.

"Okay, Joe and Bryson… you two head up to the room with the mirror, lay in the bed and do some EVP for about twenty… Christian and I will stay and see if we can get anything else in the parlor."

"I'm not sure about that one," Bryson said.

Joe chimed in nervously. "I'll go up, but not in that bed…" he laughed.

"I'm sure…" I stated sarcastically, "We'll all take our turns… Christian and I will switch with you in twenty minutes."

Although Bryson and Joe had been on several investigations, they had never been on one that had started with such initial activity. I felt the energy in the house even as I spoke to them and I was sure they were picking up on it too.

"Bryson… Joe…just stay on the two-way and if you need me call me." I assured.

The teenagers headed up into the darkness while Christian and I stood in the parlor to begin our EVP session. I traded Christian the camera for the EMF detector and began.

"Captain Townshend," I paused between queries allowing ample time for a response, if there were one. "Are you here with us tonight? Was that you with us in this room earlier? …is there anyone else here with us now?"

I continued EVP until noticing that Christian was holding the Sony infrared camera tilted as he peered toward the wall between the pump organ and the artificial seasonal

Christmas tree. I instructed him to hold the camera in an upright position, not realizing that the steady cam feature was engaged, already self correcting the angle of the frame.

"Christian, what are you looking at?" I asked as I turned in the general direction to where he gazed. There was silence for a moment and then he said:

"Something is here."

I walked toward the Christmas tree and the EMF detector burst into action. I found that a child's metal runner sled sitting near the tree actually seemed to be electrically charged. I looked carefully to see if it was being touched by an electrical cord at any point. It didn't appear so, but I slid the sled out a bit further into the room and moved the EMF toward it slowly. Again the detector went off...

"This is odd," I thought aloud.

Meanwhile, Bryson and Joe were upstairs at work in the bedroom doing EVP with the mysterious mirror. They both opted to timidly sit on the very edge of the bed as they conducted their session including pleas to move the marble in the ghost trap. Twenty minutes later, I grabbed my two-way.

"Brys, Joe... stay there we're coming up for the switch."

Christian and I entered the bedroom to find the other guys still tentatively sitting on the bed.

"Did you get anything?" Joe asked inquisitively.

"More strange EMF readings in the parlor... take a detector with you and see if you can duplicate it, ok?"

Christian and I took our posts lying in the bed as the two others headed downstairs. Another half hour, after which I nearly fell asleep, and we took up in other areas of the house. Many additional personal experiences occurred during the evening some of which we were able to debunk. For instance, on his way downstairs Joe swore he saw a black figure moving across the dining room through a doorway. We later wrote it off to an optical tracking illusion based on a mannequin with a black dress in the corner of the dining room. In other words, as Joe came down the stairs, he obviously

The Dining Room Mannequin that appeared to move

moved from right to left giving the mannequin the illusion of movement through the doorway about fifteen feet away. I duplicated Joe's trek down the stairs with the above in mind, and I must admit, that in the darkness, the mannequin did appear to sweep from left to right. This is something about Seul Choix Pointe lighthouse that I should mention. In the keeper's quarters there are a few mannequins dressed in period garb that illuminated in moonlight add to the unsettling nature of the location. I reckon this to the illogical fear some have of dolls or inanimate objects; these mannequins evoke the same gut reaction. It reminds me of a previous trip here when Bryson got a shock while shining a light through a basement window when a mannequin's head seemingly appeared from nowhere. It "kind of popped out" at him he said. I had to laugh.

Another debunking took place after Bryson and Joe sighted a mysterious glow that seemed to move independently above the pump organ. We later determined it to be a very unusual play of light off the red infrared LED on the camera and double reflected in a mirror and a window. It took us awhile to duplicate this effect and when we were finished it was 11:50 PM, and time to get ready for my lockdown. As a habit, I like to start lockdowns at midnight being that it is the "witching hour." A lockdown is a sole hunt by an investigator in the most active or creepy spot in a location. In the case of Seul Choix Pointe, this spot is clearly the basement where Captain Townshend was embalmed. Usually, these sessions will last between twenty and sixty minutes, depending on the investigator and the activity. Bryson, Joe and Christian would get some chips and pop in the HQ while they charged batteries. After that, they would sweep the Seul Choix and Maritime rooms while I sat down by the vat attempting to contact the white bearded spirit of the house. Joe walked me down with a light as I opt to do lockdowns in total darkness as flashlights can be a temptation when sitting alone in the blind. I was confident that after finding my spot, I would be able to see well enough to get back with the infrared camera. I also carried a digital camera, a two-way and an EMF detector. Joe followed me into the basement and after a couple of wrong turns, we found the vat. It is a metal sink on the wall about five feet wide and two feet deep with a separation basically creating two different containers. As I explained the embalming process of the Captain to Joe, I believe we both imagined how naturally a body would lie on top of this firmly supported sink. I believe Joe may have actually pictured the corpse as he turned quickly back toward the stairs.

"Good luck David, I'm heading up."

"Get on the two-way when you get charged hey?" I called after him.

Chapter 10

CN: My favorite part of the hunt was waiting to find out what happened on my Dad's lock down.

And so, the lockdown began. I checked the time on the camera. It was 11:59; just seconds until the witching hour. "That's what I call perfect timing," I thought while I checked baseline in the many rooms surrounding the tub

on the wall. The circuit box was located about twenty feet or so from the sink and was dead to the EMF, which was good. There was a small tool room directly behind the wall where I planned to sit on the floor. The vat would be about two steps directly in front of me. Suddenly, there was a loud bang and a whirring sound which I immediately realized was the furnace kicking in. Even though I knew where the noise originated, the sound still surprised me. It is like standing and watching a toaster at work. Even though you know that the toast is going to pop soon, when it does, you still jump. I sat down, and started snapping photos off left and right. Checking my infrared camera, I noted well over two hours on the battery.

"Ok Captain, it's you and me."

I started the EVP work talking specifically to Captain Joseph "Willy" Townshend. I planned to swing my conversation at the end of the shift between the Captain and William Blanchard the assistant and subsequent keeper. Perhaps because William Blanchard, a local, resented the appointment of this proper and disciplined British Captain, it seems there was no great love lost between he and Willy. There has even been a tale that has floated about that puts William with the Captain at the time of his death, but being unsubstantiated at this point, I won't elaborate.

Suddenly my head jerked up at the noise of something bouncing on the floor directly above my head. It sounded as though a marble or an iron ore pellet had been dropped and  bounced several times. I was startled and baffled to say the least, but then I remembered the rest of the team was at work upstairs. I took out the two-way radio.

"Hey Guys... I told you if you drop something, let me know!" There was a moments pause, and then Joe on the two-way radio.

"We didn't drop anything."

"Well, someone just dropped something on the floor right above my head," I said agitatedly. Another pause.

"David, it wasn't us," Joe responded resolutely and in the background I could vaguely hear Bryson say:

"We're clear on the other side of the building."

"Yeah," Joe quipped in. "We're clear on the other side of the building!" And the broadcast went dead with a short static burst.

I sat quietly for a moment digesting what I had heard. Quickly, I raised my camera to snap a photo to the left and then the right. I realize now that this was to alleviate the chill I had just felt with some short blast of light. Perhaps I half expected to catch someone next to me. There was nothing. I sat alone in the darkness for several minutes listening as the furnace cycled on and off to my side. Continuing to do periodic EVP work, I laid the EMF detector up on the tub where I could see its light. Hearing it would be no problem.

"THWACK!!" I held still for a moment… breathing very slowly. What was that? It came from upstairs again, but from a far distant part of the building.

"That was us, David," Joe blurted out. "I dropped the two-way, sorry."

"That's alright, it's good to know where those sounds come from," I made an effort to be more forgiving than I was with the first noise and yet firm and encouraging enough to assure the method stick. "Where are you?"

"Same room as we were before when we talked."

"You mean when I heard something drop over my head?" I said.

"Yes Sir," Joe responded, "Same room."

"Ok," I breathed into the two-way as I quickly put two and two together. There was no way that the sounds came from even remotely in the same area. There had been something above my head and this new "thwack"… yes, I said "thwack" (this is as close to the noise as I can describe) was distinctly remote. This was definitely two different sounds and two different locations. I started my EVP work with renewed vigor.

"Captain… why are you still here?" I asked. "Did something horrible happen here that I should know about?" I alluded to the stories about Townshend's embalming.

"Captain Townshend, or can I call you Willy?" I spoke, "the light on the tub and the thing that I hold in my hand are electronic devices. If you can come near and touch them, speak to me or if you can give me some of your energy, these tools will recognize you and will let me know that you are with me."

144

At this point, my battery with nearly two hours of charge went totally dead. I had no option but to call the fellows and ask for them to bring me a replacement.

"Hey guys, my battery is dead, I need another one quick."

Rock, paper, scissors.

"Ok," Joe responded. "Meet me at the stairs."

"I can't see to get back to the stairs," I said agitatedly. "Just bring it to me ok?" I sat quietly for a few minutes waiting for the cavalry to bring me a new battery.

"I'm at the bottom of the stairs David," I heard Joe speak quietly as my radio and the EMF detector sputtered to life. "I have the battery."

"Well," I said. "Can you bring it to me?"

My radio lit up again. "I'd rather not," Joe responded.

I knew then that Joe sensed something in this basement that he wanted little to do with. After dozens of investigations with the UPST, and to this day, the basement of Seul Choix Pointe Lighthouse is the only place that Joe has refused to go. I worked my way back toward the stairs while ducking to avoid hitting my head on the ceiling. Paranormal investigation in Michigan basements is not healthy for those over six feet tall. After two wrong turns, I finally saw Joe's lights.

"Thanks, stick this other one in the charger and I'll be up in a few minutes."

Well, I must say, it had been an interesting investigation to this point and we were only half way through the night. I still sat in front of the tub where it was likely the Captain had some attachment and I conducted intermittent EVP work. Realizing the cool concrete was permeating the clothing into my rear end, I grabbed a small scrap of foam insulation that was within reach to sit on. I had by this time noted that the EMF detector was picking up my infrequent two-way transmissions, so I kept radio use to a minimum. Suddenly, I heard a sound behind the wall where I sat prone. It was in the tool room and sounded like a light screwdriver or some other device hitting the floor. I immediately crawled to my feet, cold legs, butt and all. I turned back toward the entry and the short hall that would take me into the room. Through my infrared camera, I could see the electrical panel on the wall that sat adjacent to the door of the shop. I moved to the doorway and peered inside. It looked exactly the same as when I had addressed it earlier. Scanning the floor with my camera, I saw nothing out of place. I would double check this later in our video analysis to ascertain that whatever I had heard was on tape. (It was audible). I walked out and back toward the vat where I had been sitting.

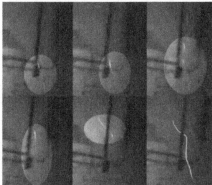

5 Frames of Infrared video with the 6th displaying digital tracking

"Willy, I said, "Can you show me with some kind of energy that you are with me?" It wasn't until six months later that I picked up an orb flying upward in front of the tub on this same piece of tape.

I am not a big "orb" aficionado, but they can be entertaining, even if not supernatural. Remember, this was January 31ˢᵗ there were no insects and had I stirred up dust it would have shown at other times in the video. It wasn't until even later, during the next winter, when my son

Christian pointed out that the orb flight pattern looked a bit like the outline of a man. As I sat in the cool basement of the Seul Choix Pointe Lighthouse, I saw nothing of this. I silently waited out my lockdown time and headed back upstairs.

***

The rest of the team had some curious personal experiences, including cold spots, noises, etc. but nothing to write home about. We made one last full team sweep around the keeper's quarters and Joe and Bryon decided to call it a night as it approached 3 AM. Christian and I had opted to stay the evening sleeping in a bed that was infamous for having the covers pulled off of you. After bidding half the team a goodnight, I went about charging batteries and getting ready for the remainder of the hunt. Christian and I did one last sweep of the facility, making sure everything was in place and double checking all doors were closed and locked. With the batteries finally ready, I grabbed the infrared camera and we headed upstairs.

"Oh shoot," I said leaning over the infrared camera on the tripod next to the bed. "I forgot the EMF detector. It must be downstairs…I'll be right back."

Christian, who without a second thought had continued to get our bedrolls out, was already in bed and nodded his head in accord. I walked down the shadowed stairwell in search of the EMF detector. Where was it? It almost seemed that Bryson and Joe had hidden the tool. After several minutes I found it under a Dill Pickle Chip bag and headed back upstairs. I stopped dead in my tracks. There was a voice coming from an upstairs bedroom. I quickly realized it was my son.

Chapter 10

"Thank you for letting us stay here Captain Townshend," Christian spoke aloud. "The bed is very comfortable..."

I smiled as I entered the room. "I'm proud of you my son," I laughed. "You didn't miss me at all."

Christian not knowing I was standing in the doorway looked up abruptly and smiled.

"I was just talking with Captain Townshend," he continued and his face showed an insight far beyond his years. "I feel comfortable here... I feel at home."

CN: I remember talking with Captain Townshend in the bedroom. I thought I could hear him talking back.

***

The night did not go uneventfully. I had two personal experiences, initially being awoken by the sweet, yet repugnant odor of cigar smoke. I felt for Christian on my left side and he still slept soundly. Rolling to my back, I peered through our room to the open doorway across the hall. As my eyes gradually focused, it seemed I could vaguely make out what appeared to be a black shadow about the height of a man moving in and out from the right side of the door. I slowly reached down to the side of the bed to grab my infrared camera. Clicking it on in one deft movement I lifted it level with what I thought I had seen.

"Is anyone there?" I continued to hold the camera in position for about two or three minutes. Had I dreamed it? If I had, it was an enjoyably vivid dream. I sat the camera down and sleep overtook me.

***

The next morning, Christian and I awoke with the sun. Before we went out to take post investigation video and pictures, we packed our gear up in the bedroom. The first thing we noticed as we turned the corner into the hall was the closet door ajar. *CN: At first I thought that someone else had been in the house. I didn't get that it was just me and my Dad.* I had specifically closed every door in

the home and locked those that led to the outside. What? We began our morning post hunt. Although the cigars had not moved, the marble on the ghost trap in the room where I thought I'd seen the shadow had moved an inch and

a half. It could not possibly have been moved accidentally. Bryson later told me that when he and Joe had done the first rotation he had noticed it and had worked for several minutes attempting to figure out how and to debunk the movement. Again, something in a remote part of the house occurred when the four of us were together and not there. As we worked our way through the facility this morning, we would later find that every door was open or unlocked. I had heard nothing but the wind. *CN: I will go back to Seul Choix because it felt like there is more there... more to discover.*

Christian and I made our way up one last time to take in the view from the top of the lighthouse. It takes your breath away. The Seul Choix Pointe Lighthouse investigation had been everything we imagined and more.

There was a mist rolling in knee level from both sides of the trail. I supposed this was common at night in the mountains of Haiti.

This was not my first trip as a missionary to this strange and mystical country and I had resolved since my first visit to avail myself of all local customs and religion. In the future, I visited the country alone and stayed with the natives in a hammock tent for weeks before the arrival of my mission team.

"I think this is it," I spoke aloud but quietly for the video camera I was carrying. "I think this is the trail that John and Jeremy showed me earlier today…"

I'd met John Josil and Jeremy Bertrande earlier that day.

At first, I was a bit wary of the young men, but they had soon earned my trust. These young Haitians had invited me to a religious service which I could not turn down. I had not brought a flashlight but the foot trail through the jungle was easily followed. It still got dark early here in January, and I hoped I was on the right path.

Suddenly, the BANGING of drums broke out in the jungle not fifty feet from the trail upon which I walked. On the video you can hear my breathing halt as I held my breath and hoped I'd not been seen. The drumming coming through the jungle grew louder.

"Holy …..," I whispered breathlessly into my camera… " I think I've walked into a voo doo ceremony."
– The Island of Hispaniola. Haiti, 6:55 pm

150

11

The House of Ludington

Case Study II

It is still cold on April 25th in the Upper Peninsula of Michigan. Tonight the UPST was taking on what, since my youth, had been a shrine of good taste and prestige in Michigan's Upper Peninsula: The House of Ludington in Escanaba; also known as the "Great White Castle of the North." Joe, Betty, Bryson and the others were unavailable this evening. Our crew tonight included Tania Belanger, Rudy Lawrence, his friend Sally and of course, Christian and I.

The owners, Ed and Suzell Eisenberger had been on my radio show "Hidden Agenda," and had spoken of the rich history and haunting of the House of Ludington. Built in 1865, this beautiful location boasted hidden stairways, ballrooms and even the first enclosed glass elevator in the state of Michigan. This one hundred and fifty year old landmark has hosted the powerful and famous since its construction. Dignitaries like Henry Ford, John Phillips Sousa, Prince Bertril of Sweden, and Cornelius Vanderbilt Jr. have all stayed here. Entertainment elite like Guy Lombardo, Patricia Neal, Johnny Cash and even today's stars like Randy Travis have adorned the long halls of the House of Ludington. The dark side of the guest list includes gangsters like Jimmy Hoffa and Al Capone, the one time king of the underworld.

At one time in the history of the hotel, there were nearly 100 rooms to let, but through the years, with some of these rooms being renovated and many being converted into suites, the House of Ludington now lets out under twenty a night.

As a boy, I recall staying with my family for an evening at this turreted tome of history. Even as a child of 8 or 9, I recognized the palpable ties of this hotel to the past. From the elaborate ornate ballroom to the simplicity of the washroom basins; history comes alive on a trip to the House of Ludington.

***

The five UPST team members here tonight sat down to a hearty meal in the Lud Pub prepared by the staff, and Suzell took the time to wait upon us personally. Ed also slipped by a few times, so the conversation ebbed between the great food and the history of the facility. *CN: I agree, Good Food!* Understand, that this hotel being built in the same year that the civil war ended and Abraham Lincoln was assassinated added an air of gravity to the history that surrounded us. I have seldom visited a haunted location older or with more history than this jewel of the north.

With dinner finished, we prepared our equipment in a room that Ed had prearranged for us on the second floor. After we had all the cameras, recorders and tools loaded with new batteries or recharging, I grabbed a video camera and the five of us joined Ed for a pre-hunt walk through of this huge building. The first floor of the hotel was divided between the ballroom, the Emerald Dining Room, the King George Dining Room, the Lud Pub, and a two room gift shop. There was also a large area where Ed, Suzell and their children, Kallie and Wyatt have called home since 1996. Ed told accounts of recent spirit activity in the ladies bathroom on this floor. There is something about the vulnerability of being in a bathroom and realizing you are not alone that is unsettling. I was already thinking "lockdown."

***

My Father Rudy had a good local recall of the hotel's history and Ed was very well informed, fielding questions left and right from all of us. *CN: the House of Ludington is a monster building and after visiting other Al Capone spots in Chicago, I like the mobster history.* Ed started us out on the ground floor of the hotel, taking us through the dining rooms, pub, ballroom, etc. The history of what was originally called the Gaynor House and later rebuilt as the House of Ludington is almost too much to digest. Ed showed us through the basement and kitchen areas as we discussed the famous people who had stayed at the hotel including Alphonse Capone. Having visited Alcatraz on one of my trips to San Francisco, as well as the site of the St. Valentine's Day Massacre in Chicago, I was particularly interested in Capone and his association with the House of Ludington. For those of you who aren't familiar with Al Capone, he was the leader of a Chicago crime syndicate during the prohibition. Moon shining, prostitution and gambling rackets garnered Capone (also known as Scarface) a virtual mafia empire. He was later finally apprehended not for the violence, but for simple tax evasion and was housed at the infamous Devil's Island (Alcatraz) off the California coast. The history of Capone in Michigan is extensive. His relationship with and later suspicion of the Purple Gang from Detroit is the stuff of legend. It is said that the Purple Gang had all the territory east of Hwy 131 and Al the west. This made the mafia's control of crime in Michigan nearly absolute. In other words, what they wanted to manage they did. This was until the New York originated Purple Gang brought two Capone exiles from Chicago into their fold. The era of good feeling between the two competing forces then soured. Yes, Al "Scarface" Capone had more than one tie to Michigan. Visits to the somewhat desolate Upper Peninsula possibly as

Capone   Dillinger   Nelson

an alternate route returning to Chicago are many and well documented (called the back door). It is also whispered that other notorious criminals like Baby Face Nelson and John Dillinger have used the Upper Peninsula as an escape route.

Ed told us about an elderly gentleman who had stayed in the hotel actually played cards in the tower with Nelson. The fact that Nelson and Dillinger were members in the same gang lends credence to these stories.

Capone not only frequented the House of Ludington, but also owned a private residence in Escanaba. Many local communities in the Great Lake State claim the mafia kingpin owned a residence, mansion, hotel, etc. etc. in their community. Most accounts are simply urban legend as Capone never bought anything under his own name but the countless sightings give the stories a tone of belief. It is rumored that Scarface Al Capone would reserve the whole third floor of the House of Ludington for his gang when they were in the area. Another tale ties the later popular owner of the Hotel, Pat Hayes (originally from Chicago) with Capone. Could Al have tipped Pat off to this beautiful business opportunity? Truth and imagination seem to meet at the House of Ludington. Ed told us of the "secret" stairway that led from the office in their quarters which, he and Suzell believed, may have been built for a speedy escape in case of a police raid or other incident during the prohibition. There was even said to be an underground tunnel that led from the House of Ludington to the Escanaba harbor. It was supposedly used during prohibition and blocked off in subsequent years. Whether or not all of these tales are accurate, traversing the same hallways that a murderous thug like Al Capone had walked was not only exciting but a bit surreal.

Ed decided we would continue the pre-hunt upstairs, so we boarded the elevator to the second floor. As we ascended I wondered who in the past had ridden in this same compartment. This level of the hotel is graced with a period barber shop display as well as other décor indicative of the early twentieth century. On the second floor, our headquarters was near one of the stairwells. This was the room that Christian and I, if necessary, would sleep this night. There are also two staircases located on opposite ends at the front of the hotel and one at the rear. The other access is of course the exterior glass enclosed elevator near the entrance built in 1959. As we gazed over Lake Michigan's Little Bay de Noc, although unspoken, we all understood that investigating the House of Ludington would indeed be a treat.

***

Ed, by this time, had left us to our own devices. Before he'd gone, he had told us that there were a few rooms vacated on the second floor but that the third floor was empty. After our first sweep, Rudy and Sally took off around midnight leaving Christian, Tania and me the House of Ludington to ourselves. In addition to our flashlights, the equipment we carried was 2 infrared video cameras, 1 mp3 recorder, an EMF detector, 2 digital cameras and an infrared thermometer.

Immediately out of the door of our room, the EMF was off the charts. It seemed to become particularly prevalent as we neared the staircase. Our earlier baseline reading had been non-existent. All we could do was watch and wait until it turned off. We stood at the top of the stairway, and as I moved to and fro, I was able to discern the hotspot as the top few stairs and the landing of the second floor. After several minutes, the beeping abruptly stopped.

"Wow," I said. "I haven't seen it go crazy like that

since the Paulding Light."

"Yeah, that was kinda' freaky," Tania voiced. "I felt like there was something here earlier."

Tania moved past me to look more closely at the top of the stairs. Christian had taken a few steps away from us and had focused his digital camera down the dark hall that ran adjacent to the west stairway. I heard him whap off several pictures in succession.

"Do you see something Christian?" I asked.

"Just shadows, but it's like they're coming out of the doors."

We walked to the hallway across the building from our room and peered down the corridor. I declined to  mention earlier that Ed had told us about an incident in room 205, which was down this same section. The customer told of the fear she had felt during the night, some months ago, when she had heard her doorknob clicking as it rolled back and forth like someone or something had wanted in. We will place a static cam down this hallway after our first couple of sweeps during the night. Later, when I searched online, I discovered many accounts referring to this floor including a young lady who actually witnessed a full body apparition in her room. The man was dressed in very proper period clothing standing near her bed. Recounting that the spirit appeared to be a waiter or some kind of hotel staff, she swore it was not a dream. Another neat little tidbit that I found was from another paranormal team that had visited the House of Ludington. They have posted video of this same hall and although the video was not conclusive, the lady who took it believed that she had seen "heads sticking out of the doorways." We moved back to the east stairway near our room and made our way down to the first floor.

***

Not since hunting Fayette State Park had the UPST been to a place with so many visibly different areas to hunt. Each room had a history of its own. Some of the hotel had been rebuilt after the original Gaynor construction and the west wing wasn't added until 1910. Our EVP work ranged from speaking to staff, to Pat Hayes, to any spirit that might be lurking.

"Mr. Hayes," Tania spoke aloud in the North bar which featured a huge fireplace and much memorabilia from the Hayes era. "How do you feel about the renovations going on here at the hotel?... We think they're beautiful."

We all stood mute for several moments when abruptly the silence was punctured by a bump near the rear of the structure.

"That could have come from the kitchen," I said. "Somewhere back by the restrooms."

"Isn't that where Ed and Suzell live?" Tania asked as we worked our way through the tables toward the source of the noise. I illuminated the route with my flashlight as I tried to pinpoint the location of the bump. The kitchen was too far to the side for it to have come from there, I realized as we got closer to where from the sound had come from.

"Ed and Suzell live further back behind where I thought I heard the sound." I continued. "Did you hear it?"

"I did," Christian acknowledged.

Tania concurred. "I heard something that kind of sounded like a chair being sat down."

I nodded in agreement and added, "Or a door lightly closing."

By now we stood in front of the ladies bathroom where the most recent activity had been. We entered the two stall cubicle, which was tastefully decorated in typical women's bathroom manner. I say this because, although I have not been in many women's restrooms, I have noted over the years that if a budget of $20,000 dollars goes into restrooms and décor, the men's room enjoys a healthy five and a half bucks. I guess we men are more focused on the job at hand and I seldom recall asking my buddy Paul to accompany me to the bathroom. Again, I digress. The ladies room had a huge mirror and what appeared to be a comfortable lounge chair all surrounded by beautiful ornate wallpaper; just the atmosphere to help get you in the mood to void. If there had been cable piped into each of the stalls, it would have been perfect. I made these observances out loud to the others and Tania got a kick out them. We sat down on the settee and began our EVP work. Christian began.

"Why are you here," he said then paused. "Do you like sitting in here?"

I had to chuckle at this point. How do you do EVP in a lavatory? Normal lines of questioning like "why do you like it here and what do you do here?" become potty humor very quickly. Tania said it best.

"What do you ask... hey, why are you hanging out in a john?"

We all chuckled and I decided it was time for my lockdown.

"Why don't you and Christian hit the second and third floors and I'll do a lockdown here for another thirty minutes or so," I said.

The two of them agreed and headed upstairs as I maintained my posture on the settee periodically panning my camera around the bathroom and toward the mirror. Although I did occasionally have an internal feeling that something or someone was watching me  from near the entrance, I had nothing more than the personal experience of a chill. The later analysis of the video bore this reality out. After about 35 or 40 minutes, I stood and opted to say my goodbyes before I found the others.

CN: ***When you were locked down in the ladies room at the House of Ludington did you go?*** The answer is no, I never thought about it at the time but this action may have evoked some activity… next time I will make the effort. This query also leads to a better point. When you are involved in an investigation with a haunted restroom facility, what do you do with your static infrared? The UPST uses a "flapper." All this device entails is a piece of cardboard taped to the top of your camera. When privacy is required put the flapper down, but remind your team to swing it back into the open position when they are done.

***

I had reached the third floor where I'd thought Christian and Tania were working but I didn't see them at all. The corridors of the upstairs level were dimly lit by the exit signs near the stairwells and the shadows loomed over the long halls so completely you could barely see to the other end.

"David here… where are you?" I spoke into my two-way radio.

Tania responded. "We're on the second floor, where are you?"

"I'm on the third floor." I spoke.

"Come down to the back stairway," Tania said. "You have to see this."

I was not far from the front stair, so I took the steps down. Walking past our room, I noticed the light was on. I stuck my head in and took the time to switch out batteries on my infrared camera. Turning off the light I looked down the long murky hallway to see Tania and Christian standing silently at the far end. I made my way to them.

"What is it?" I whispered in a low monotone to Tania.

"Just listen."

The metal door that the two stood in front of was opened about three inches. As we stood there, I faintly discerned something that I can only describe as a low baritone resonance; a tone that was almost human, but not quite. *CN: Tania heard a humming and asked if I could too? I was sure I could and she called my Dad to come and hear.*

"It's the door," Tania pointed toward the crack. "It's… like… vibrating."

I trained my infrared camera on the opening and moved resolutely toward the doorway. I reached out my hand and felt the door. There almost seemed to be warmth to the metal door and perhaps a vibration but I am not certain. What is certain is that the door was the source of the note we heard. As I touched the exit opening, there seemed to be audible ebb in the tone of what we heard. I

161

quickly ran through the options of what might cause this strange phenomenon. A settling of the building?... sure, but not leading to one continuous tone and still settling after a hundred and fifty years? Could it be a piece of machinery  running downstairs and the vibration making its way up through the substructure? This was a possibility, but we had been downstairs and I had noticed nothing running that would have pulsated to the extent needed to come through two floors. We would check out the basement in short order to ascertain what machinery might be running. In the meantime, we stood in awe of this weird occurrence. If it is not the distant echo of a mechanical vibration, perhaps it was the little seen phenomenon of resonance. I believe what we had here may be something akin to a tuning fork responding to a sound that we cannot hear or isolate. Miners, deep in tunnels, searching for iron, gold or other metals have sometimes noted resonance and vibration exuding from the actual rock. Tuning forks will resonate in response to a pitch that is unheard by the human ear. Just what is making this door sing is the question.

***

We now walked the west wing of the second floor. In low monotone voices we conducted typical EVP, tossing out the names of dignitaries and staff that were known to have stayed or worked here. We walked the full length of this barely distinguishable hallway and then turned back toward the front of the hotel. I marched in front with

Christian following and Tania bringing up the rear. The three of us continued to spout EVP queries as we moved down the shadowy tunnel that was the corridor.

"Stop," Tania said from behind us. "Listen to that." She stood two doors back and was looking up at the ceiling of the hallway. Christian and I stepped back to where Tania was anchored transfixed on the ceiling. She looked at me, "Don't you hear it?"

Christian quietly nodded and said, "Music."

We all stood silently, listening into the emptiness. It was there, very clear and definitely coming from upstairs.

"Its music, but it sounds more like a party," I supposed. "I can hear voices too… like in a bar…" Now, as many of you know, I have traveled for years as a professional musician. I know the sound of a lounge, and this is what the noise reminded me of.

"Is it a TV?" Christian offered. *CN: It sounded like a party to me.*

"I suppose it could be if it were muffled just right, or a radio," I answered. The sound of the music and voices was mysteriously muffled; almost "other worldly." Had it been a television, I believe it would have been a clearer sound. Kind of like a television through the floor of a hotel…. right? As for the programming, it would be interesting to find the channel that played music and party noises for five minutes straight. I suppose there could be an AM radio station that provided this distant sounding programming, but this did not answer the most important issue. I continued:

"It could be a TV or radio, but there are a couple of things against these options. The first being that Ed said there was no one on the third floor."

"That's right," Tania agreed.

We stayed here for several minutes making sure that we had an audio record of the musical party sounds. As we  started up to the third floor to see what we could find, all I could think was that maybe Ed had made a mistake about the vacancy?... if this were not the case, we very possibly had some interesting data. When we trailed the ghostly melody to the room directly above the second floor area where we'd heard it, the room was empty and as dead as the grave; pun intended. I would address this anomaly with Ed tomorrow.

***

We went back to our rooms on the second floor to re-charge and to grab a quick snack. The beef jerky and Coke was the perfect mixture to renew our vigor for another sweep. We decided to hit the basement and as we left the rooms, the EMF again blasted into life at the top of the stairway.

"Well," I exhaled. "At least the spirits are consistent."

"Oh, I almost forgot!" Tania looked toward Christian and directed him to me. "Christian, show your Dad what you found in that room."

Christian was digging for something in his pocket with a mission. He suddenly held two items in his hands. The first a chess piece; a white bishop made of plastic in the Staunton design indicative of the 1970's.

"Where'd you find this?"

Tania informed me that she and Christian had been in a room a few doors down from our HQ. They had inspected the room thoroughly before they began doing their EVP work. Out of the blue, Christian noticed this chess piece lying in plain sight in the middle of the floor as though it wanted to be found, but this wasn't the most interesting find.

"Look at this Dad." Christian said as he held out his other hand. In it was the photograph of a man taken in 1894!? *CN: I remember finding the picture on the second floor in a room that was being fixed. I didn't see it when we walked in but when I turned around, it was just there. I knew my Dad would like it.*

"David, I swear this wasn't on the floor when we checked the room out." Tania prefaced the discovery. "We did our EVP work and Christian said what's that, and there it was right next to where we'd picked up the chess piece."

I looked at the photo quickly and put it back in our room not remembering it for over a year. It ended up being accidently stored with our equipment, a gift given later to Ed and Suzell. The photo was about 2 x 3 inches and was a tin type on thick cardboard stock. I looked carefully at the picture and could make out the photographer, Sophus Nissen. This portrait had been taken overseas in what appeared to be Vestigrade, Mariebo, which I would later find out, was in Denmark.

We could also vaguely make out a name at the top of that may have been the man in the photo. Fesiwig Tatevcev? It was obviously in the care of an immigrant or visitor that had the wherewithal not only to have the picture taken in 1902, (not an inexpensive endeavor), but the ability to pay for a room in the House of Ludington; the Great White Castle of the North. Absolute identification of this man in the picture would be a challenge. I would later find out that Nissen was a popular photographer in Denmark. I was able to make contact with his great, great nephew who is also a photographer, via internet. He told me that the Dane had sold the studio but thought he may still be able to contact the owner (yes, they were still in business in 2012) to see if they kept the old records. The photograph had a serial number on it that and if the 120 plus year old records had been kept, it would be easily traced. As of this printing, I have heard nothing further.

The face card was somewhat degraded but still in surprisingly good condition for over 120 years old. Nearly twenty hours were needed to digitally enhance the photo and he looks alive; I wonder what he did for a living? did he have a wife and children? Many unanswered questions, but this is part of the historical excitement that is paranormal investigation. Here is the computer enhanced photograph:

***

Now we were in the basement and our search for the running machinery that would have created the "singing door" proved fruitless. We also checked that the kitchen was silent; it was. By now it was after 3 AM and we were running out of steam. Tania opted to make the long trek back to Newberry on the eastern side of the Upper Peninsula and Christian and I to stay put for the night. After our mandatory UPST hugs (yes, I am told I'm a hugger), we bid Tania goodbye and I set a static infrared camera in the west hallway shooting on room 205 and a good deal of the halls expanse. Christian and I rolled down the covers of the bed, laid down and passed out.

***

The sun streamed through the drapes that sat to the east of the bed. It was a cold, but sunny day in the Upper Peninsula of Michigan. I arose first as sun and sleep do not mix for me... too many days slept through in a room of total darkness after a late night playing music I think. The equipment was quickly packed, including the static cam that had run for about three hours in the west hallway.

The House of Ludington seemed deserted this early morning, so instead of waking our gracious hosts Ed and Suzell, I chose to write a note. I told them of the sounds from the third floor and asked if I had heard correctly that there were no tenants on this level. The morning was brisk as Christian and I packed the equipment in the car taking with us the unforgettable experience that had been the House of Ludington investigation.

***

Ed later confirmed that the third floor was empty.

*"Can you see it?" Robert asked us in a low but
excited monotone voice, "right in front of the sign."*
Robert Declercq, Gregg Masters, Christian and I were on the cold
fourth story marble floor of the Asylum. The black mass slipped back
and forth sometimes obscuring the illuminated EXIT sign about one
hundred and fifty feet down the shadowy hallway.
Gregg responded, "Yeah, I see it, but what do you think it's up to?"
Christian had been in a side room and I had directed
him to come out and see this rare event.
"Dad," Christian whispered. "I'm a little creeped out."
This was the first time I had ever seen my son show
any sort of trepidation. In fact, in last year's calendar, for "scariest
moment" he had answered: None Yet.
*"Come here," I said grabbing his hips and pulling him onto my lap.
"I don't want you to miss this."*
We sat silently, witnesses to this shadow figure as it slid to and fro
keeping its distance at the end of the hallway. Five minutes passed and
I'd finally had enough. I felt through the blackness to find Robert, and
handed him my infrared Camera.
*"Here Robert," I said as I lifted Christian to the floor between
he and Gregg. "Keep it on me."*
I stood up and walked into the darkness.

– Trans Allegheny Lunatic Asylum, West Va. – 12:15 am

12
The Helmer House Inn
Case Study III

The locations covered in the following two chapters are but eleven miles apart and both have important elements worth mentioning to the aspiring ghost hunter. The Helmer House Inn is located in Helmer, Michigan and is a registered historic landmark. For many years, it was closed and then renovated into a bed and breakfast. The Jolly Inn is located in Germfask, Michigan and in its past has served as a boarding house and tavern among other things. We will begin with the historic Helmer House Inn.

***

Chapter 12

The Helmer House Inn was built in 1881 to 1882 by Reverend Mills, a Presbyterian minister, as a parsonage and mission house. In 1888, Gaylord Helmer, an enterprising businessman, bought the structure and turned it into a general store and hotel. He called it the Helmer House Inn. An extension to the building was added, and in 1894 it became a stagecoach stop and Helmer added a post office. The Inn was sold again in 1904 to Charles and Jeannie Fyvie who ran the business until 1950 after which it sat deserted and fell into a state of disrepair. The post office had already closed in 1914 when Lakefield Township  became RFD (Rural Free Delivery). Dr. James Fyvie renovated this historical building in 1981 just in time for its centennial, and it was declared a Michigan Historical Landmark the following year.

The Helmer House Inn was sold again and became an upper scale restaurant with period settings and a bed and breakfast. The current owners are Tuffy and Jody Burton. For many years this beautifully renovated locale was the destination for every romantic dinner and weekend in the area. But with the advent of the change in the political climate around 2008, the Helmer House, like many businesses saw revenue decrease and they closed their doors.

I drove by the building many times over the years aware of the ghost stories espoused by the staff and ownership who once worked this bustling business. It became apparent that this would be a good time to address the owners with a request to launch a UPST investigation.

The Burtons were amazing people, eager to relate stories, legend and lore about this beautiful Inn. Their daughter Holly, having had several personal experiences was also most helpful. Through the stories told by the family I gathered that the consensus of guests, personnel and ownership felt that the spirit haunting the Helmer House Inn is Gilbert. Affectionately referred to as Uncle Gilbert, this was a man who had worked the business for the Fyvies. It seems that Uncle Gilbert has a propensity for females, often tugging their hair, touching them on the shoulder, etc. He either has no interest in men or simply prefers the ladies. I was told of strange episodes, similar in nature and experienced by different employees. These people while closing the restaurant late at night would see an elderly man sitting at a table through the service window, but after walking out to the floor to tell him that the Inn was closed, would find an empty table and an empty restaurant. The sheer number of witnesses to this type of occurrence makes the Helmer House Inn a potentially prime paranormal destination.

***

It is February 2010 in Michigan and sub-zero temperatures had to be taken into consideration for the investigation. *CN: It was only fifteen minutes and I already thought about asking my Dad for a car break to warm up but I know him. I put up with it.* The Helmer House Inn had not been heated or had electricity for nearly a year and would be very frigid. Dressing warmly was not a choice, it was a necessity. The UPST travels with a Coleman lantern for light and in this case the warming of our hands at the equipment table which we located on the ground floor near the entry. We also carry a dozen or so pocket hand warmers that are made of chemicals that react with an electrical charge from a small disc within. These pocket warmers can be purchased at most sporting goods stores and are re-usable by simply boiling them back to a liquid state.

Extra batteries as well as DC/AC invertors would be employed in vehicles so that we maintained battery life throughout the night. We decided to keep one of the cars running so that there would be a warm shelter for those who needed to gain some body temperature. I did not wear my pink shorts for this investigation. Our equipment for the investigation included 4 infrared cameras, 3 EMF detectors, 2 Mp3 recorders, 1 infrared thermometer, 4 digital cameras, dowsing rods and flashlights.

It was about 9 PM and Tuffy Burton, arriving shortly before the team, had already opened the Inn. The UPST hunters included Betty Lustila our researcher, Dave and Margie F., Joe Leduc, Bryson Lawrence, Christian and I. Joe and Bryson quickly laid out the equipment and I grabbed an infrared camera to follow Tuffy as he showed us through the building. The Inn's first floor had a large pantry, a spotless kitchen and an L shaped dining room that was attached to a smaller more intimate dining area. The restaurant looked as though it had been open just that evening. The tables set, chairs and tables neatly aligned and glasses upside down just waiting for a splash of wine. There was even a huge dry erase board with the specials from the last working night. As we rounded the corner that led to the upstairs bedrooms, I heard Tuffy say:

"Whoa…what do we have here?"

I caught up quickly with the owner as he stood near the base of the stairs. He was staring at a two foot square picture that had broken its glass, obviously having fallen to the floor.

"That's strange," Tuffy said. "The last time I was in here this was up and there hasn't been anyone here since autumn."

I looked carefully at the fallen landscape and then noted the empty spot that it had once occupied. I had actually witnessed this very phenomenon before at other haunted and deserted locations. Looking closely at the wall I was not surprised to discover the nail on which the picture hung was still in place. Whatever had caused this picture to crash to the floor also would have had to lift it up about 3/8 of an inch to coax the anchor up over the nail head; interesting indeed. Before we explored the bedrooms, Tuffy grabbed a broom and we removed the glass so as not to interfere with the later route of investigation.

At this time, Tuffy showed us what I consider the hidden jewel that is the Helmer House Inn. He opened a door to a sitting room gorgeously outfitted in early 1900s  décor. This room was used as a waiting area for the overflow that inevitably occurred on weekends and holidays at the restaurant. I recall eating a special Valentine's Day dinner here years before where I enjoyed the wait in this classy setting room nearly as much as I enjoyed the delicious meal. And for those of you wondering, Yes, I was even then making plans for the UPST to visit this bed and breakfast.

Chapter 12

In fact, I believe I may have annoyed my date by asking too many "Uncle Gilbert" questions of our pretty waitress.

The upstairs rooms were wonderfully kept, some with common bathroom facilities typical of the era and others with private accommodations. After imparting more tales of full body apparition experiences and physical contact with female employees, Tuffy left us to begin the hunt.

***

The investigation began with Joe and Bryson taking one bedroom and Dave and Marge F. another. Betty opted to stay in the bedroom at the top of the stairs where she and I had felt a chill on the pre-walk through. Earlier in the evening at about the same time,  Dave F. had captured some orbs on his digital camera and had informed me that he thought this room may be a hot spot. This later seemed to be confirmed by the dowsing rods which could not help but cross at the top of the staircase just steps from the room. Christian and I had the ground floor to ourselves.

I could hear the others upstairs settling in for some serious EVP work as Christian and I walked the restaurant, pantry, and kitchen before finally sitting in the dining room.

"Uncle Gilbert," I spoke to empty air, "If you are here with us, please go ahead and talk... this box in my hand (I referred to the infrared video camera) can hear you and we will relay any message you would like to give us."

Christian jumped in. "You must like how nice the restaurant is, don't you Uncle Gilbert?" The words were barely out of Christian's mouth when we heard a voice from upstairs.

"Oh... Oh," I recognized Betty's tone from her nest at the top of the stairway.

"Come on Christian," I said moving quietly but quickly to the stairwell. We made our way up the steps, stopping on the landing and peered into room 6. There was a heavy feeling in this room that was perceptible.

"Who is that?" the hushed voice came from the upstairs room.

"It's David and Christian."

"Something just touched me." Betty lay on her side in the cold bedroom.

Christian and I stood quietly as Betty described physical interaction with the spirit we referred to as Uncle Gilbert.

"I was going though the regular EVP questions," Betty said. "And I asked if he could touch me. I thought it was my imagination at first, but then he did it again."

I could tell by the look in her eyes that this was no joke.

CN: I knew Betty had been touched because we had been on lots of hunts before and I hadn't seen her this way.

"Where at?" I asked.

Betty described two brushes on her cheek, both in response to her communication. Betty was calm, but understandably appeared a bit shaken.

Chapter 12

"Shouldn't we leave the camera with her?" Christian chimed in.

"How about you take a quick pop (soda) break downstairs with Christian," I spoke quietly to Betty, "and I'll sit in here with an infrared."

Christian and Betty headed to the lower level where the rest of the team was now moving to their second posts. I carefully positioned the infrared camera on the basin that sat near the door and trained it across the room. As I lay on the bed that Betty had just vacated, I placed an EMF detector visible to me on a chest near the end of the bed frame. I began the conversation.

"Uncle Gilbert, I know you like ladies and I am *not* one…" I decided to try a different tact as I emphasized my "not." "So I am *not* going to ask you to touch me…what I am going to do is ask you to touch the red light that I have on at the end of the bed."

I sat silently for a moment looking at my equipment when I heard an audible click from my camera on the wash basin. Looking closely, I noticed that the red infrared LED was off. "What the?" I thought silently. Rising, I walked to the camera and was stunned to discover it off? I flicked the camera on and was relieved but befuddled to see a full two hours of time left on the battery. The camera had simply

 turned off by itself. Could it have been the cold? No, I didn't think so, we have had cold weather hunts before and these Sony cameras have always been super reliable. This had never happened

before. I placed the camera back on the sink and again lay

down to continue my EVP work. It was then that I looked at my re-seated camera that I realized.

"HEY... the infrared camera has a red light too!"

When I had asked Uncle Gilbert to touch the red light, I was referring to the EMF detector, not even taking into account the fact that the infrared camera has a red LED as well. Could I have just had an interaction with Uncle Gilbert? After a few minutes I headed down below to find the rest of the team. I saw no one. Where was everyone? The Helmer House is not small, but not nearly large enough to separate a team of seven people. As I walked the full length of the restaurant, camera in hand, I had an almost surreal feeling of detachment. My first thought is the team was playing a trick on me. I turned corners saying aloud: "Ok, I know you're here... not funny."

For what seems at least ten minutes (and was probably only three). I looked through the lower level and even out at the cars. Had they been abducted? It was then that I heard voices from beyond the kitchen. The different squads had hooked up and did a session in the pantry/storage room. I laughed as reality again overtook me.

***

The hunt continued until it was about 2:30 in the morning and the cold had permeated our bones. We packed the equipment and warmed up our cars. As we took one long, last look around the Helmer House Inn, we wished the owners good fortune with giving the historical past of this beautiful Inn a new future.

"Hold it a second Christian," I whispered sharply.

We came to a complete stop at the center of
the cemetery in the middle of the night.
Out of my peripheral view I swore I'd seen a shadow
skirting us moving parallel, to my son and I, near the road.
I believed that within this "shadow figure" I had actually
discerned individual arms and legs. Very carefully, I raised
my infrared camera, quietly turning toward the location
where I had observed the figure.
Nothing.
"Ohhhh," I exhaled disappointedly, *"… did you see that
Christian?"*
In a nonchalant, matter-of-fact sort of way Christian
responded:
"You mean the guy with the hat?

"

- 2007 Pit Stop and Fairview Cemetery Investigation, 11:54 pm

13

The Jolly Inn
Case Study IV

The Jolly Inn of Germfask, Michigan has become an iconic representation of the typical Yooper tavern in the great white north. As I type the word "yooper" in my document I note that it is underlined as though I have made a spelling error. Well, for your information, "yooper," referring to those of us who inhabit the Upper Peninsula of Michigan, is now (according to Merriam Webster) an official word of the English language, so take that Microsoft. They won't get it out in west coast San Francisco but what do they get?

The Jolly Inn has become a staple of tourist entertainment during the four season year in the UP. The food is good, the beer wet, and the owners friendly. I became aware of the activity here as a lad listening to stories of the Jolly Inn and the Wonder Bar, (across M-77 and now torn down). I remember an old saying from my childhood that I always found amusing in regard to this popular bar: "Jolly Inn, Stagger Out." My interest was furthered when I interviewed author Jan Langley on my radio show "*Hidden Agenda.*" She was on plugging her book *A Ghostly Road Tour of Michigan's Upper Peninsula.* In it was a story about the haunted Jolly Inn and the ghost that the owners past and present called "Captain Jolly." I decided to reach out to the Tovey family, local townspeople who now owned and ran the Tavern and Restaurant.

I called Glenda, a friend of mine and now the manager of the Jolly Inn. Her son Damian owns the facility and she and I worked out a night that the UPST could investigate this haunted tavern. She told me on the phone about several incidences, recently and over the years; not only sightings, but doors rattling and other kinetic activity. One cook actually had spaghetti thrown at her hitting the wall near where she was working at the stove. A picture was produced of what appears to be a fog at the bar behind one of the bartenders. The staff here viewed this photo as confirmation of a paranormal entity. I also interviewed a previous manager that had actually lived upstairs. This woman related how she'd become frightened many times after closing at the sound of someone trying to get in through the front door. Nearly all of the employees have had an experience of one kind or another. They never felt alone and one young staffer even refuses to close up alone at night. All of this, in combination with a mysterious telephone call received on the restaurant's answering machine, led to what might be a very active hunt at Tovey's Jolly Inn.

***

"Get out of there!"

The voice was low and sounded garbled as though almost otherworldly. The telephone number that this threatening message had come from was unknown and received when the renovation began. It may have been a hoax but led to the intrigue of the hunt nonetheless. Glenda showed us through the Jolly Inn. Many spots of interest were displayed, including, the stage area adjacent to the main dining room, the kitchen, the tavern, the basement and the upstairs that in the past had once served as boarding rooms. The renovation of the facility was in its midst which inevitably leads to a spike in paranormal activity.

***

Glenda left team UPST to our own accords. On this investigation were: Betty Lustila, our researcher, Joe Leduc, Bryson Lawrence, Rob Giles (resident skeptic), Lori Bennett, Tia Miller, Christian and myself. As we charged batteries and readied our equipment, a couple of the team played a game of pool in the tavern. I encouraged this activity as I felt it would be beneficial to recreate the normal bustle of the locale as closely as possible to when the regular haunts occur. A cue-ball ghost trap logically followed the pool game.

On this investigation our squad carried 4 infrared cameras, 2 EMF detectors, 2 infrared thermometers, 2 Mp3 recorders, 4 digital cameras, flashlights, cross-hair and bulls-eye style ghost traps and a computer. We immediately broke into three units with Rob and Joe on the ground floor, Bryson,

181

Chapter 13

Lori and Tia in the basement. Betty, Christian and I headed upstairs.

***

Bryson's team of Lori and Tia sat in the basement listening to the muffled footsteps from above. They attempted to conduct EVP recording during the down cycles of the furnace, but it wasn't warm in this shadowy basement. Tia and Lori were feeling chills and they weren't sure if it was atmosphere, activity or temperature. Bryson made sure the ladies stuck it out for the full shift.

Rob and Joe were running the ground floor conducting EVP with an Mp3 recorder. Rob had taken it upon himself to personally debunk the photo that Glenda had shown us earlier. He took multiple photos at different angles hoping to capture a similar optical illusion. Since the photo had been taken, the no smoking law had come into effect in the state of Michigan, so duplicating the fog of a smoky bar was out of the question. Unfortunately, this reality left Rob's debunking half completed; Thank you liberals.

Christian, Betty and I had settled on a couch in one of the upstairs rooms and were also conducting an EVP session. *CN: I remember being upstairs with Dad and Betty and she had a cell phone app. that kept saying "devil" and "red barn" limited to only scary stuff, but still kind of freaky."* Christian sat between us and was rolling through a menagerie of questions for whoever might be listening. During a lull in the inquiry, Betty spoke in a hushed voice.

"Christian, hold on for a second."

There seemed to be some undercurrent of voices nearly imperceptible from the corner of the room about six feet from where we sat. I stood up and moved to the wall between the window and the couch.

"It sounds like ten people talking all at once," I said.

Betty responded, "That's exactly what I heard."

"I hear them too," Christian chimed in for good measure. *CN: I thought it sounded like a commotion in the bar downstairs.*

I took out the two-way radio to address the team directly below us, "Hey Joe, were you guys just talking?"

There was a short pause and the radio sputtered to life, "Just EVP."

I turned around in a full circle to figure out if I could still detect the voices from the same direction. It seemed I could. I decided to leave Christian and Betty and move on to the next room for another audio test.

"Look there you two," Betty pointed from the couch toward the rear of the second floor. "I just saw a light over there."

I turned in the direction Betty indicated but saw nothing. I took two steps toward the back rooms with infrared camera filming everything in hopes of capturing anything.

"Now it's gone," Betty declared.

"That's interesting," I thought moving backward and to my right in an attempt to again sight the light that Betty had seen.

"There it is again," Christian announced from his position next to Betty.

"I don't see it," I said and repeated my steps toward the earlier indicated location. "What color is it?"

"Red," Christian and Betty both offered simultaneously.

I laughed as the reason behind my midnight disco dance abruptly dawned on me, "It's the LED on my infrared camera."

It seems the wall between the rooms was partly removed as renovation was ongoing. A thin veiled curtain had been run between the rooms creating an eerie red glow in Christian and Betty's room when the infrared hit it.

***

Meeting back on the restaurant level, we compared war stories and in particular the voices we heard from  behind the couch in the corner. Joe and Rob confirmed that they had engaged in a short conversation while staging the ghost photo debunks, but they believed that was minutes before my call to them on the two-way. Bryson's team also confirmed having had a conversation regarding EVP and the cold spots, but he couldn't pinpoint when. It was then that I recalled seeing old photos of structures in Germfask, Michigan being built in about the same years as the Jolly Inn. Back when "Pine was King," the studs in an old building like this often ran from the ground up two or three full floors. I am sure this added to the stability of the structure, but the unknown side effect of this type of construction is its conduciveness to sound and vibration. Our idea regarding the voices evolved into the theory that both lower floor teams were engaged in concurrent conversation which reverberated through the very building itself. We would test our theory during the next two shifts.

***

We had all taken our first rotations on every floor and now we broke into different teams so that each of us had a chance to walk with the others. Betty, Lori, Tia, Christian and I initially took to the ground floor and set up our second ghost trap. We had become aware of a story during the research stage about a child, just eight years old, who had been struck and killed by a motorcycle in 1978. It seems there was a softball tournament in town and the boy was left outside in the car while his Mother went into the Jolly Inn. Finally, the child lost patience, ran across the road to get her and was hit by a motorcycle. We have his name, death announcement and an eye witness, but I won't relate all of this here as his family still lives in the area. I felt this was an excellent tie in to the sound of the door rattling late at night and I had an investigator of the same age who, tonight, was going to attempt communication with this poor young boy.

"Christian, grab your toy car that I told you to bring."

I spoke to my son as I laid a cross-hair ghost trap on an empty table top in the bar area near the door. Christian walked up to me dragging the toy car out of his front trouser pocket. He had been prepped before hand for his EVP and I had asked Christian to simply speak to the boy as he would one of his friends.

Chapter 13

I carefully sat the car in the dead center, (no pun this time) of the ghost trap. After photographing the car and trap from above, I had Christian sit at the table and start speaking to the young man, who coincidentally was named Christopher. Here is yet another example of using a "chrono-trigger." That again, is an item, sound, smell, etc. that appeals to the time period or targeted spirit. *CN: I hoped that the boy that died would like my matchbox car and would talk to me.*

"Hi Christopher," my son began. "My name is Christian."

I had positioned an Mp3 recorder on the corner of the table that Christian now occupied. I videoed the first few minutes of the EVP session and since Christian was comfortably conversing with empty air, I thought I would go to the back kitchen and visit an empty walk-in freezer for a lockdown. Perhaps a young entity would be more inclined to speak with my child if he is alone. I announced my exit and walked to the kitchen.

"No problem," Christian mumbled and went back into his conversation. "Do you want to play with my car?"

I entered the dining room and informed the three girls, who were exploring the stage and asked them to come get me in twenty minutes. Although the freezer was not on, it was chilly inside and darker than dark. As my eyes adjusted to pitch black, the blinking battery light at the rear of my camera actually seemed to illuminate the small cave. After about 10 minutes of talking to myself I realized that if my EVP were to be successful, I would probably be conjuring the spirit of a dead pork chop or something. Nevertheless, I stuck it out until Betty knocked on the door. Everyone was sitting around a dining room table eating what had remained of our snacks.

"Get anything?" Rob asked.

"Cold," I replied.

***

By the time we finished our last two rotations, it was 2:30 AM. Betty, Rob, Lori and Tia said goodnight leaving Bryson, Joe, Christian and I to finish up. I had the guys position 2 static infrared cameras at both ends of the building while I unpacked the laptop. I sat it at the table where Christian had finished his EVP work an hour or so earlier and opened up the music that I had downloaded. One item I'd found of particular interest during my discussion with an eye witness to young Christopher's death was the irony of the song playing on a nearby car radio: Billy Joel's *"Only the Good Die Young." **CN: The most fun I had was when my Dad started the music and we played pool before we went to sleep.*** This had given me an idea for the chrono-trigger we were about to employ to end our investigation. I had recorded twenty tunes that were hits the year of the death and just before; songs that had received a great deal of airtime and were still in rotation. I started the music as the rest of the team laid out the sleeping bags and stretched out. On a side note, when I posted this video on YouTube I found I was in violation of copyright infringement for this barely heard background music. Do yourself a favor when you post your videos and always list them as for "educational" purposes, which of course, they are.

***

We slept as the camera's rolled. I have been asked often "what are the regular sounds that cycle throughout your sleeping hours?" My patent answer is: "it's the ghost of a lumberjack sawing logs." The sun rose and so did what

was left of the UPST. Parting notes include the fact that the voice phenomenon was not repeated during the night and implausibly, the Mp3 recorder that I'd left with Christian recorded, but nothing other than static. In addition, although there was no door rattling this evening, we found through our research on Captain Jolly that his being the spirit that haunts the Jolly Inn is unlikely. Mr. Jolly was not a Captain and sold the tavern years before his death. He bought a farm, died outside Germfask and is buried in Manistique, Michigan. The more likely being to haunt the Jolly Inn is probably a well known local personality who frequented the establishment nearly every afternoon. This well loved man was not only born on the premises of what is now Tovey's Jolly Inn, but had a heart attack and died there. If I were a gambling paranormal investigator, my money is on him. ***CN: I think there is something more at the Jolly Inn to investigate.***

All in all, the Jolly was a great hunt. Friendly staff, awesome renovated surroundings and on my visits there since, great food too! The UPST will return.

"The only thing that could have moved it would be
an animal like a raccoon or something."
I addressed Robert Declercq and Christian who stood on the balcony
in what was previously the sanctuary of the Sedamsville Catholic
Church. Christian and I had set a bulls-eye ghost trap earlier with a
Chinese ball positioned on this upper level in a remote area. This ball
actually rings when it moves. Obviously, no one had stepped into it or
they would have heard it.
Robert responded,
"Yeah, raccoons would play with anything shiny like that."
The silver ball had moved at least four and half feet...
This was too good to be true! An object moving mere inches is
rare if experienced at all. Almost two hours later I joined
Christian, Mary, Diane and Robert.
"Dang it!"
I exclaimed entering the rectory kitchen after leaving
my lockdown in the sanctuary.
"What's up?" Robert asked.
"I just saw a friggin' raccoon!"I sighed.

– Sedamsville Rectory, Ohio, 1:45 am

190

14

Nahma Inn
Case Study V

The Great Lakes have more than their share of haunted lighthouses and deserted towns. The northern shore of Lake Michigan is a treasure trove of paranormal activity and where the Sturgeon River meets Big Bay de Noc sits Nahma. Its location at the mouth of this river led to its naming from the Chippewa (Ojibwa) word for sturgeon: *Nami.*

The Bay de Noquet Lumber Company out of Oconto, Wisconsin founded Nahma in 1881 as its Upper Peninsula base of operations. Nahma was a model company town designed as the point of business interaction between the buyers, shipping and the logging camps supplying the hardwood. The evolution of the community progressed with the creation of a common square and a grand boulevard. These civil improvements led to the construction of the Nahma Hotel in 1909, which is now called the Nahma Inn. In the seventy years that the Bay de Noquet Lumber Company ran the village of Nahma, they had a thriving community even establishing their own railroad, the Nahma and Northern which ran over seventy five miles of track from town to several logging camps. In 1951, Nahma had outlived its feasibility as a lumbering town and was sold that it might become a summer resort. The American Playground Company from Indiana, the purchaser, lacked the capital to bring the resort dream to fruition. For those interested, *Life Magazine* published "*Sold One Town*" in July of 1951 which gives many interesting details on the sale of Nahma.

The Inn is owned by Charley and Laurie Macintosh, who not only have rooms available but a lounge with live entertainment and a first class restaurant that will amaze. ***CN: I like the Philly Cheese Steak Sandwiches!*** The Nahma Inn has been immaculately restored and every visitor through the front door can easily imagine having taken a century long step into the past.

Legend and ghost stories abound at the historic Nahma Inn. I sat with Charley and Laurie on my pre-hunt interview where they related tales of glasses in the bar area being moved and even thrown by forces unknown. Spectacularly, these kinetic events have sometimes occurred in front of several customers who have all sworn to the activity. There is a consensus that some of these goings-on can be attributed to Nell Fleming, a local school teacher and company secretary who also did part time work at the hotel. Also in play for the activity is Charlie Good, the initial supervisor of Bay de Noquet Lumber Company. Charlie, born in Nahma, now commuted from Chicago, and made frequent trips to Nahma, staying at the hotel. It is rumored that he and Nell had a relationship that in the end was unrequited leaving Nell heartbroken. Additionally, a green apparition approximating the height of a girl or short woman has been sighted in the main hallway on different occasions by totally independent parties with no knowledge of the activity. Footsteps, odors, knocking and eerie vocal music have actually brought some witnesses to tears as the emotion of the experience was overwhelming. It appeared that the Nahma Inn is very active and the time had arrived for the UPST to become the same.

***

Two weeks later, Christian, Joseph, Bryson and I arrived before the rest of the UPST to set up equipment and to prepare team grid locations. Charley helped us organize the various gear in his business office as the regular Saturday night clientele began to arrive at the popular destination. This type of location is what the UPST terms a "Life Active Hunt." On very extraordinary occasions, a paranormal investigation can and should be conducted with

a high level of human activity. The Nahma Inn is one of these rare cases where a crowd does not interfere with the activity and may in fact elevate it. A number of incidences have taken place within full view of the regular bar patrons and apparently interactively. Our plan is to draw on this energy for the first half of the evening before we go silent to extend our EVP and investigative umbrella.

We are joined by the full team with Robert, Mel, Jason, Linda and Tony Caron, as well as the Raymond's: Craig, Brenda and Audrey. Others investigating cadet's such as Wendy Jo Kinn, Missy Yaklyvich, Danielle Dobson, Kim Stafford, Jimbo Harnois and Sara Fried also take part.

Charley and Laurie have also kindly made the adjacent General Store available for our investigation (another building they own). This huge two story turn of the century store is stock piled full of inventory from the 1950's and earlier. It is a treasure trove of history for the paranormal investigator  and in fact was featured in an episode of *American Pickers* on the History Channel. *CN: Yeah, I remember that show... they called Nahma (Nay-ma), "Naaahma."... Charley was nice not to correct them.* Our team number this evening has been orchestrated to cover several different locations but the shear area offered by both the Inn and the General Store will stretch the limits of the UPST. The empty expanse of the store will offer an opportunity for solitary and quiet investigation before the Inn empties and we perform quieter investigation there. The equipment we are carrying this evening includes 7 Infrared Video Cameras, 6 Mp3 recorders, 2 Infrared Thermometers, 3 EMF detectors, Laser grids, Obelisk, Spirit Box and, of course, flashlights and two-ways.

"I'm telling you that we smelled it at the same time."

Brenda swore to the incident that she and Audrey had experienced minutes earlier. I was skeptical, in part because the investigation was still in its first swing and also because the Raymond's were recent UPST Academy graduates and still in the midst of their first few hunts.

"Okay," I said. "Give me the details."

The Raymond's related the tale of entering *Nell's Room* and settling down to do EVP work. The detail that they gave me soon alleviated my cynical nature and I was very proud that I had trained these investigators. They told me that our online psychic, Eileen Bathory, mentioned that she had sensed someone in the room just as the odors became apparent. ***CN: I have been on many hunts with her and we talk about what I see.*** WIFI technology is useful to paranormal investigation in many ways, including quick online searches and remote viewing by interested team members and fans. In addition, the UPST has found the internet particularly helpful in the participation of psychics and mediums in virtual investigations with us. We use Skype, which is a free program that displays video and audio both ways with the online assistant actually being carried about on an internet capable tablet. This technology has led to astonishing results in the past and is something continued with qualified individuals to this day.

As was mentioned before, the Raymond family also related that they had become aware of a strong fragrance in *Nell's Room*. Brenda wasn't certain but thought the odor was similar to burnt sandalwood. Audrey stated that she thought it smelled like lavender.

"Yes Audrey," Brenda interjected her agreement. "You're right…that is exactly what it was… lavender!"

I sat with the Raymond's for several minutes before leaving the room to find my way downstairs and outside for a cigar. On the porch I met Laurie; owner and chef.

Laurie asked me, "So, did you get anything yet?"

"Well," I replied. "We did have an interesting incident… Audrey and Brenda think that they smelled an identifiable scent in Nell's room…"

Laurie stiffened and spoke abruptly, "Don't tell me… lavender."

"Yes… yes… that is exactly what they smelled," I happily confirmed. ***CN: I was not there but this is pretty cool.***

This was pleasing news. It seems this is a common occurrence and many of the Inn's employees have smelled the lavender odor in Nell's room; Laurie was not surprised. And from the UPST's perspective, I prized the fact that Laurie had no further information other than a "scent" had been present, after which she nailed the specific odor. This is what I consider substantial evidence of  an event; whether paranormal or natural. Our mystical Nahma voyage had begun on a great tact!

***

Robert Declercq had taken a team over to the General Store and was experiencing noises that although probably natural (building settling or shifting with the weather) seemed to be almost responsive. While Robert hunted the first floor with his squad of Christian, Mel, Jason, Danielle, Kim and Jimbo, I was upstairs with Linda and Tony Caron, Sara, Missy and Wendy. Melissa and Jason's team had been on the second floor about half an hour earlier. They'd made some interesting discoveries, including store accounting dating back to the late 1800's. This confirmed that business actually began before much of the town's highlights like the hotel had even been built. Jason also alerted us to the fact that their team had happened upon an actual electro-

shock machine. ***CN: We had been here and seen it before, but I didn't know it was for shock therapy.*** Many of us hadn't seen this type of device, whose modern image has become one of torture intended for the mentally ill.

"Okay," Linda said. "That definitely creeps me out."

After nearly 45 minutes I sent my upstairs squad back to the Inn and continued to check out the second floor alone. As I have said before, solo lock downs are not for the faint of heart but if you have someone with experience on your team willing to investigate an unusually creepy spot alone, often times this may elicit activity.

"If there's anyone here with me right now… make a sound please." I spoke as I walked slowly toward a window where the full of the moon dimly illuminated a checkerboard pattern on the floor at my feet.

"THWACK."

Something had hit the floor between where I stood and the entrance stairway to this area. I moved back toward the center of the room but found nothing. I still felt obligated to respond:

"Thank you for letting me know you are here," I spoke to open air as my camera battery went totally dead.

***

"What?" Robert looked at Christian and Mel inquisitively.

"He just started acting funny," Christian reiterated, "and then he ran out."

"He what?" Robert grunted in disbelief having to hear it one more time.

Melissa said, "I don't know exactly what happened… we were in the office doing EVP and the next thing I know I hear the door slam and Jimbo is gone."

Robert grabbed his two-way radio barely containing his bewilderment.

"Robert to David." The two-way radio in my pocket squawked to life breaking the silence and jerking me to attention. I reached into my UPST hoodie and extracted the two-way.

"David here," I was now sitting at the south side of the second story near the stairway. By now my flashlight was dead as well as my infrared camera. "What's up Robert?"

"You aren't going to believe this," Robert responded. "Harnois just freaked and ran out!"

I can't help but smile when I recall Robert's vocal tone, instantly discerning that he was between annoyed and amused. By now I was thinking it was about time to call in a rescue team. I again yanked the radio to my mouth.

"Hey Robert, tell me more about it in a minute but right now, come and shine your flashlight up the stairs so I can see... my batteries are dead."

Christian and Robert met me at the base of the steps and described what had happened to our errant team member. About ten minutes into the ground floor sweep Mel, Danielle and Jason had began their EVP work in the office. More than one remote knock and several bumps were heard by the group. One member even thought she had heard voices from across the room. It was about this time that Jimbo began to get progressively agitated. He paced nervously back and forth between teammates repeatedly asking:

"Did you hear that? ... Did you hear that?"

"The next thing I knew, the girls told me he was gone," Robert added.

Later on we discovered that Jimbo had made it back to the Inn and was visibly shaken. *CN: This was so weird! I've seen people freak out on the Ghost Hunter's show, and I have had the same feelings, lots of times, but I have always stayed. I felt sorry for him.* Linda related that he'd told her he had felt a presence, began to feel suffocated and nauseous, opting to escape the General Store before he got

199

sick. When I finally got to Jimbo, he was feeling better but he had several questions regarding what had happened. It seemed he had never experienced this type of spiritual oppression and was simply not equipped to handle it. After talking with me for about twenty minutes, Jimbo felt as though he could continue, and promising not to desert his team again, rejoined the squad. The UPST doesn't advocate an investigator staying in any situation or location where they feel imperiled, but on the other hand if you have this type of experience, be absolutely sure to let your teammates know before you leave a hunt.

***

As the investigation progressed, many personal experiences were logged by the UPST in addition to what we considered reliable evidence. I was privy to another personal experience that was significant. One interested patron approached me as he was leaving and reported seeing an unexplained figure in the hallway at about 1:00 am. He told me that from his seat in the lounge he was monitoring a service window that led into the hallway. He had just gotten up to see if his wife had finished in the restroom when his glance through the window caught what he thought was her coming back into the tavern. Rounding the corner into the hallway he was surprised to see no one there.

"I'm telling you I saw a woman in the hall," he proclaimed, "and then she was gone."

"And you thought it was your wife?" I asked.

"Yeah," he continued, "I was waitin' for my wife to get out of the bathroom and thought I saw her there through the window when I was goin' to the hall."

"How tall is your wife?" I was very aware of the spirit that was said to frequent the hallway and wanted to establish whether or not this was indeed a short person the man had seen.

"She's right over there." He said pointing to a table in the tavern.

"What is she?" I queried, "about 5 - 4?"

"Not even…" the man chuckled, "maybe 5 foot 2 if she's lucky."

"But it looked like a regular normal person?"

"From what I could tell," he said. "I just saw the brown hair, went around the corner and she was gone."

I thanked the man for his input, gave him a card and invited him to join us at a UPST academy in the future. It

is unfortunate that we did not have a camera on the hallway at this point but we did level a static camera later when someone leaving the bar would not accidently bump the tripod. On an aside, static infrareds were installed in the bar area, *Nell's Room*, hallways down & up for the full night.

Perhaps the best piece of evidence we procured that night at Nahma was not gained until about three weeks after the investigation. In a discussion with our online psychic she revisited the moment entering *Nell's Room* via Skype on a handheld tablet.

"I saw a man in a kind of suit standing near the door… dark brown hair, thin mustache, weak chin…I think his name is Charlie," she said.

"Could you draw a picture of what the man you saw looked like?" I asked.

She said she would try, but what the psychic didn't know was that since the investigation our researcher had actually come up with some obscure photos of Nell Fleming and Charlie Good and had emailed them to me.

This photo of Charlie was actually taken upon his induction into the military for World War I. Other than this single photo, I had never seen an image of Mr. Good as a young man or with brown hair. I had only seen him with what appeared to be snow white hair, so I was curious when discovering that she had pictured Charlie with darker hair and a mustache. I secretly videotaped this conversation as I waited for the portrait that the psychic was drawing to be completed. Needless to say, I was pleasantly taken aback by the results. This sketch was presented to Charley and Laurie and is now at the Nahma Inn. Did she see Charlie Good in *Nell's Room*, or did she see the photograph in my head? Either way, I include it here so you can make up your own mind. So, after you've done that and you'd like a different kind of paranormal experience including great food, lodging and entertainment, the UPST highly recommends the Nahma Inn!

Christian evokes activity by writing a note with his ABC's at a deserted orphanage.

"Go ahead and start your EVP work up on the stage,"
I spoke quietly.

Christian and I stood in the darkness of the Emperor Room
in the historic Palmer Hotel of Chicago.

"You have a really nice ballroom here," said my son.
In the hours preceding our exclusive access to the Emperor
Room, we had already visited the reportedly haunted fifteenth
floor and viewed hundreds of portraits of entertainment stars
that hung in the hotel's corridors. Christian had by now taken
the stage of this beautiful and ornate ballroom where entertainers
like Bing Crosby, Bob Hope, Rita Moreno Frank Sinatra and
Judy Garland had performed in years past.

"My sister played Dorothy in the
Wizard of Oz at her school Miss Garland,"
Christian continued. "I hope you don't mind."

– The Emperor Room of Chicago's Palmer Hotel, Illinois, 11:55 pm

15

Fayette

Case Study VI

Shelton Hotel

For this case study, I have decided to include the highlights over several investigations and UPST Academies at Fayette Historic State Park, in the past known as Fayette Ghost Town. This may very well be one of the Upper Peninsula Spook Team's favorite destinations due to the abundance of activity and the sheer size of the deserted settlement.

Fayette came to be in 1867 as an industrial community located on Lake Michigan's Big Bay de Noc. Between 1867 and 1891, this thriving village produced 229,288 tons of Charcoal Pig Iron that would be shipped to Chicago and elsewhere all over the country for the manufacture of steel. At one time, Fayette had nearly 500 residents, saloons, an opera house, and even a brothel just outside of town. Jackson Iron Company halted operations in 1891 due partly to the decline of the charcoal pig iron  market and the growing scarcity of hardwood that was used to fire the huge blast furnaces. After a couple of attempts around the turn of the century to transform this small picturesque village into a vacation destination, the town was virtually abandoned. In 1956, Michigan declared Fayette a historical site and it became a state park in 1959. It was also added to the National Registry of Historical Places in 1970.

Fayette State Park now has over twenty different structures either partially renovated or in museum display mode. Sheer rock cliffs and Lake Michigan surround the buildings that nestle around the one time heart of the Fayette; the blast furnace. The picturesque nature of Fayette combined with the abundance of history make it one of the finest vacation and historical destinations in the country hosting thousands of visitors every year.

***

It was a brisk autumn day in Michigan's beautiful Upper Peninsula and its Spook Team had met at the welcome center of the historic Fayette State Park. Most of the team was there including our Detroit wing led by Robert Declercq, with Mary Gisslander, Kyle and Dana. Betty Lustila, the UPST researcher and resident chef had put together a beautiful spread of Roast and vegetables along with hors d'oeuvres, chips and coffee. She was ably

The Family Guide to Ghost Hunting

assisted by Sara Cameron, Lori Bennett and Tia Miller. Rob Giles, Joe Leduc, and Brys stuck to eating while our western Yoopers made their way to the Garden Peninsula and Fayette State Park. The logistics of this investigation were expansive and I'd called in every UPST affiliate available to hunt the nearly twenty plus building ghost town.

Two weeks earlier Christian and I had met with the Park Director Randy Brown for a pre-hunt interview. Video of our session was posted to upspookteam.info and many of the team took part in an online Skype forum where I covered different historical aspects of Fayette. *CN: I didn't know how we could do a whole town. I had been on loads of investigations and it was only one place or two. We would need a lot of people and I hoped we were up to the job.* As an extra incentive, I asked the team to conduct their own historical research and Betty and I would give an award to the most interesting story. Our two hour tour of the park was packed with interesting facts about Fayette and the end of the 1800s. Park Director Randy's point of view was one of healthy skepticism but was open to anything that the UPST might discover. My point of view was that if this village wasn't haunted, it should be.

Nearing assault time, our western Yoopers finally arrived: Melissa Olson, Jason Zupancic and Kayla Johnson had at last grabbed plates of food and it was good to see them again. As I started to go over team assignments and history, I noticed that Kyle and Christian were missing.

"Ok… where are my son and Kyle?" I asked. No one had a response as it seems that my eight year old investigator had it in his mind to display his familiarity with Fayette by means of a personal tour. *CN: I admit it… I was showing off my knowledge of Fayette… is that bad?*

207

Chapter 15

When I realized what had occurred, I grabbed my two-way to tell Christian to get back to the welcome center with these words. "This investigation will not start off with the team heading wherever they please... talk to me next time."

I had previously constructed a grid that included all team set-ups and 45 minute rotations or "swings," which I was in the midst of covering with the team as the young men arrived back, sufficiently contrite. I let the issue drop and continued our investigation preparation. After the pre-hunt knowledge that Park Director Randy Brown had given us, Christian and I further whittled down the hunt to eight prime locations which included:

- The Shelton Hotel - A huge Inn with dozens of rooms including the suite where Fayette Brown had stayed. Mr. Brown was an agent for the Jackson Iron Company and was responsible for choosing this prime site for the business. The Shelton has a beautiful view of the bay then called Snail Shell Harbor, from Fayette's second story windows and an absolutely breathtaking visage from the third floor dormitory. The Shelton Hotel is like a maze and at night you can get turned around more than once. This building sat across a two track wagon route from the Jackson Iron Company office and at one time would have been the hub of social activity and events in the village. After all, even when Professor Loomis' Canine Carnival was in town, they had to stay somewhere.

- The Opera House – A theater and music hall with a stage, curtains, backdrops, seating, etc. Entertainment in the hay day of the community varied from bands to magicians, ventriloquists and even dog acts. In fact, back stage on a wall in what once served as a dressing and prop room are the signatures of multiple entertainers who'd once performed here. The delight and party atmosphere reflected in period photographs of the Opera House clearly demonstrate its importance to this vibrant community. One small ghost story from a few years ago still follows me regarding the music hall. Christian and I were at a Fayette summer function

in 2006 and I related a story I had heard years earlier to a Detroiter standing in line with me for a soda. The story had come from a third source friend of mine in the early 1990s. He related the story of how a buddy of his from Garden, Michigan was riding across the deserted park on snowmobile. Being just after dark and chilly out, he and the others in his party stopped to say hello to "Jack Daniels." The others had ridden off while he stowed his bottle and mounted to start his sled. As the din of their snowmobiles died in the distance, suddenly he heard it. The sound of an orchestra, and it seemed to be coming from the direction of the music hall. He took a number of steps toward the hall and discovering that it wasn't his imagination, donned his helmet and gunned his snowmobile away. I was told he would not go near Fayette after this incident. As I related this tale to the Detroit fellow, I saw his eyes open with amazement: "That's my friend," he exclaimed. "My wife and I are up visiting and it took everything we could do to get him to come with all of us here... and he said only during the day!" After this revelation, the Detroiter took me to meet the gentleman and I even recognized his family name. His recounting confirmed the second hand story I had originally heard. I promised to keep his name to myself and we said goodbye. One thing that I cannot keep to myself is the excitement of investigating the Opera House.

- Number 27 - One of several middle class laborer two story buildings located on a back loop near the lake. Although not much is known about its history, paranormal or otherwise, I felt that subjecting the team to one of these structures in a natural, less remodeled state might benefit our investigation. Number 27 was in a well preserved condition but was just creepy enough to get excited about.

- The Morphine Addict's House – A building where, upon renovation in recent years, there was discovered a stash of empty morphine bottles in one of the walls. In all likelihood, enough bottles to have kept the addict in medication for many  years. The odds that this person was a tortured soul are high and the chance that Dr. Bellows would have known about it higher. In the late 1800's morphine could be sold at a drug or even general store but was still monitored by the local physician. The excessive use of this substance during the civil war had alerted the medical community to its very addictive nature, but medical knowledge of drugs, addictions and withdrawal was still limited. Opiates (like morphine) were sometimes recommended for any pain whatsoever; even withdrawal, the very effect that addiction to the drug had subsequently created.

- The Superintendent's House – This is where the Jackson Iron Company's director of operations lived. A beautiful house with servant quarters, a lovely period parlor and antique furniture set to museum

status behind glass. The UPST had researched stories describing the deaths of at least two of the Superintendent's children: Charles Rhodes lost his 12 year old daughter just after arriving. John. B. Kitchen's daughter, Elizabeth Jane died at only eleven days old. Some believe his other daughter Clara also died in the home. William Pinchin died in the first year of his service in an upstairs bedroom. It has a panoramic view of the bay in front of the blast furnaces and I confess, a beautiful setting to say farewell to the world. This room is where a four year old Christian Lawrence did some of his earliest EVP work. The parlor is periodically arranged to display these sad events, including a small child size casket set for what would have been the visitation. The covering of mirrors was traditional in the case of mourning, but primarily practiced out of the superstition that souls of the departed could be trapped within the reflection interrupting their final journey. I am aware of more than one visitor claiming the mirror's death shrouds alter between non-existent and obscuring the glass.

- The Blast Furnaces – As I have mentioned earlier these smelting kilns were the heart of this industrial community. It is said that if one is very quiet, you can actually hear the distant echo of the banging and clanging of machinery intermixed with the yell of conversation. This is what I call "the Castle of Fayette." One man lost his life while walking home in a blinding snow storm when he fell from the nearby cliff. It seems there would be ample EVP opportunity here.

- Dr. Bellow's Infirmary – The medical office where Dr. C. J. Bellows treated all the ills of the late 1800's. Obviously a location where deaths, births and industrial injury have been contended with. The bedrooms and personal quarters were

Robert installs push light

upstairs so Dr. Bellow treated the patients near the kitchen on the first floor. We will emphasize conducting EVP work with the good Doctor from a lone bed in what would have been the treatment/operating room.

- The Old Fayette Cemetery – Although this antiquated village cemetery was not probed during our first couple of investigations due to weather and time, I wanted to include it as an example of how the Upper Peninsula Spook Team respects religious tradition and human memory. On an aside, we have not missed this treasure on our last few hunts. It is very old and perfectly descriptive of a turn of the century Upper Peninsula cemetery. There is much to be learned from the names and dates on these weather torn stones. More on this later.

St. Peter's Church Cemetery

The funeral of Mrs. Julia Phelps . . . took place last Sunday, a large concourse of people following her remains to its last resting place.

Located south of the Fayette townsite, on a sandy bluff overlooking Lake Michigan, this Catholic parish cemetery dates from 1877. Today, several early grave sites are unmarked. Another cemetery, located north of the townsite, served Fayette's Protestant residents.

***

Randy allowed us to drive our vehicles down to within the village for purposes of unpacking our equipment. This evening, we set up the HQ in the Shelton Hotel, but on subsequent hunts, the base of operations would be one of two other nearby buildings: the business office or the tackle shop. I mention this because the locations become important in the absorption of future events. For the last five years, I have been conducting UPST Academies throughout the Midwest. Fayette State Park has been generous enough to allow the Upper Peninsula Spook

Team the opportunity to teach and instruct rookie ghost hunters at the site. It has become a popular part of Fayette's Fall Fest, with the last year's mini academy enrolling 126 students for discussion, training and a basic hunt. Many of these cadet's go on to take part in the full academy and to join the UPST ranks. We will get into more on the UPST Academy later.

After the equipment inventory and allocation, the second item of business was to set team assignments. I sought to keep friends, family and co-investigators together, but also wanted to mix hunting styles. In addition, I deemed a UPST trained member important to every group with a newbie and we had a few this evening. My short list  of generals for this investigation included the most experienced staff: Robert, Betty, Bryson & Joe, Mel & Jason, and the little guy; Christian. All of these people had either been personally trained by me or had double digit investigation experience. At this point, my son Christian had already been with the UPST for four years and was in excess of thirty hunts. Seldom have I led a team with any investigator boasting more hunts than my son who, on the completion of this book registers over one hundred and thirty investigations. I have learned to rely on this type of experience and attempt to find or nurture it in all chosen squad generals and instructors. It is a natural pacifying agent and easily spotted by inexperienced and experienced hunters alike.

On reflection, I would reconsider one particular team assignment. Two "experienced" investigators were brought in to fill out what would be a 22 investigator hunt. They would this night expose their religious view; atheism. I would in turn expose to them my "What the ....?" response. Needless to say, their "experience" reflected all of the thought they had put into their religion. I do not hunt with atheists, (nonbelievers in an afterlife) or muslims (where the afterlife contains no spirits but supplies 72 virgins). That would be like taking Upper Peninsula weather forecasts from Al Gore. There are sheep everywhere, but when I have investigators wandering into potentially risky locations, I prefer to leave these simpletons at home or teaching college.

***

FAYETTE I

Our course of action included a walk around with Christian and me reiterating Park Director Randy's history, hanging pop-on lights and discussing the upcoming investigation. These pop-on lights were installed at remote locations like Dr. Bellows and Number 27 where a bit of a trek was required to find them. One thing that you may have noted in reading this book is the symmetry of our *"swings"* or team rotation. This means the length of time in a room, location or building. Over the years, I have learned that whereas it is claimed the attention span of a child is twenty minutes, the maximum attention span of the average paranormal investigator is only about forty-five. This is not insulting, it is a reality gained in over forty years of investigation. Anything less is not enough to get results and anything more without activity is monotonous. *CN: Why not 60 minutes? Aren't you the one that is always saying "let's sit down?"* When I call for a *swing* and a particular team is in the midst of activity they always have the option to take another turn at their current location and the next team will jump over them. Paranormal investigations are nearly always fly by the seat endeavors and each requires a different organization and mindset. Foreseeing intricacies and problems of a hunt comes with the knowledge of success and mistake. Experience breeds experience and if you are new to paranormal exploration, I always advocate finding knowledgeable people in the field to connect with. Let me give you another simple tool: When it comes to an investigation, watching most paranormal television shows will educate you in how a legitimate hunt **should not** be organized. Look for real experience.

After going over my investigation grid and team sets,

 Robert, Kyle and Dana went to the second floor of the Shelton Hotel to set up a 4 camera infrared surveillance system while Jason and Melissa went to install another 4 camera IR system at the Superintendent's House. The rest of us drank; just kidding. The rest of the team charged batteries, allocated equipment and talked hunt details. Every squad tonight carried at least one infrared video camera totaling 8 walkers. In addition to the 2 static infrared surveillance systems employed at the Super's house and the Shelton, every team carried a myriad of additional equipment from 4 EMF detectors and 3 IR thermometers to 1 Spirit Box and 1 Obelisk. Reminiscent of many investigations this hunt seemed uneventful. The UPST performed their sweeps

throughout the night with little significant personal experience or evidence noted. The hunt and the history of this unspoiled destination were unique and although we all had a great time, we were not optimistic about the evidence. It was only in the next few weeks following the feedback from the team analysis that I realized what a success the hunt had been. Music from the Opera House, EVP from: Number 27, the Superintendent's House, the Blast Furnaces and most prevalently, the Shelton Hotel.

Mary Gisslander and Christian had decided to start early EVP work at the Shelton while the boys set up equipment. One of the tenets I instruct in the academy is "EQUIPMENT ON AT ALL TIMES." Some of our best evidence has come from these unprepared walkthroughs and Mary was well aware of this carrying an Mp3 recorder. She and Christian addressed Fayette Brown's suite while Dana and Kyle finished erecting the surveillance system.

"I have a little boy with me named Christian," Mary spoke, "did you ever have a little boy?" In the next few moments that followed you can hear the fellows far down the corridor setting up their equipment when suddenly Mary and Christian captured what may be the UPST's favorite Class A EVP:

"OH, YEAH."

It sounded as though the low gruff male voice had been delivered within inches of the recorder and he didn't sound in good-humor. This recording is absolutely pristine; there is no doubt as to what is said and that it wasn't our team that said it. ***CN: My Favorite "catch" of all time because I was there!*** In fact, when I received this Mp3 through the mail from Robert, I was at my girlfriend's cabin in the Upper Peninsula. Christian and I were thrilled with the EVP response and played it several times before the young lady cried out from her seat in the living room:

"Turn that off, it's creeping me out."

***

The first investigation of Fayette did not progress without some bumps in the road. Our track star Bryson went down for the count not even an hour into the hunt. On this particular investigation, we had made the Shelton Hotel our HQ. Before the sun had even begun to set, I noticed Brys sitting on an equipment trunk and looking a little green around the gills.

"I don't feel good right now, Uncle David."

"What's wrong with you?"

"I feel kind of dizzy and sickish," Bryson said quietly, "like nausea or something."

"Why don't you hit the truck and rest up."

I pointed him out the door. There was a strange feeling in the air. Several of the team mentioned to me that they'd sensed a "heaviness" in the Hotel. Byson ended up going down for the count. I took him water and checked on him every hour or so but for some reason this young athlete had totally crashed and burned. Today, Bryson barely recalls the investigation. Occasionally our team encounters active locations that exude an ominous or oppressive atmosphere. This reality came to conclusion in a most unpleasant manner at the Shelton this evening.

I was with Rob Giles, Tamara and Christian in the Opera House conducting EVP work when my infrared battery unexpectedly died. We had just been at Number 27 and since I had already burned a cell there, I had little choice but to retreat to the Shelton for a back-up. I walked the short distance across the gloomy courtyard to the hotel to find my researcher cousin Betty Lustila and her team of granddaughter Sara Cameron, Lori Bennett and Tia Miller sitting in the lobby.

"What are you girls doing here?"

"Just waiting for Melissa and her team to finish upstairs," Betty said glumly, "We've been listening to them walk around up there for half an hour."

"What?" I confusedly muttered as I pulled my grid out from my hoodie pocket, "Mel and Jason are supposed to be at Dr. Bellow's Infirmary...?" I grabbed my radio, "Melissa? Where are you at?"

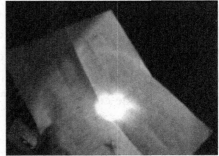

It was at this point that Betty and her team's jaws dropped and their eyes got as big as saucers. They realized that I had no other team in my grid on the second floor of the Shelton Hotel. Jason's voice came over the two-way:

"Dr. Bellow's Infirmary."

***

I had rejoined Rob and Christian back at the Opera House and we had just finished a half an hour of total silence when my young cousin, Sara Cameron, lit up the two-way radio.

"David," Sara sounded a bit anxious, "Grandma just took a digger."

"Hold on, I'll be right there."

Keep in mind, that although Betty is a "grandmother," she started her family very young and was only in her forties on this hunt. As quickly as I could move I was back off to the Shelton Hotel. Arriving there I found Betty sitting on a chair recouping. She was still a bit faint but assured me that she was okay.

"Hey David," Robert's voice broke into my medical examination, "What happened to Betty?"

"She's okay," I replied, "She just took a digger."

It seems that Betty had passed out as she walked toward one of the static infrared cameras and had fallen directly on her face. I was relieved that she wasn't hurt more badly but she was done for the night. It was only later I found out that people from Lower Michigan and the Detroit area don't really use the term: digger. In the Upper Peninsula a digger occurs when you catch a toe or trip and fall forward. Interestingly, Robert and his downstate team had come to the conclusion that "digger" meant poor Betty must have pooped her pants. Just to make things absolutely clear, she did not.

So why did we come upon so many strange occurrences at the Shelton tonight? I believe that it can be attached to a couple of things. First, the Shelton Hotel is one of the more active locations that we have visited and foreboding and melancholy seem to run hand in hand at locations like this. Secondly, I had noted earlier when we were organizing our equipment that I could smell methane gas (bat guano). *CN: I could smell something really strong that year when we walked in but its lots better now.* I am very familiar with this odor due to my working in the gas and heating field. Most times, installing or fixing a furnace in an old house is the very first work to be done before renovation. Bats are a prominent element in empty old buildings and I know the smell well. *CN: Bat Poop can*

220

knock you out! Take note... got it. I believe that the excitement of the hunt combined with methane and whatever EMF activity we were getting led to the perfect storm and took out two of my team. At about 2:30 am, I packed Bryson in with Betty and her squad and saw them off.

***

FAYETTE II ACADEMY I

As mentioned earlier in the book I have conducted UPST Academies in multiple haunted locations all over the country. The training typically includes a two hour class session with an introductory hunt. At Fayette, due to the huge numbers, I have opted for twenty minute mini sessions during the day, followed by night hunts for beginners and advanced students with the wish to get their feet wet in the world of paranormal investigation. I also bring in my trusted generals to help share the burden of what is often over one hundred hopefuls. Pulling off this type of expansive instruction requires a great staff and I am very fortunate to have exactly these people in the UPST.

It is during the first Fayette Academy that I am conducting a small group of about six advanced investigators at nearly 12:30 am. Whereas the beginner's academy hosts children and parents in the twilight hours, the advanced academy includes older teenagers and adults that may choose to hunt until morning with the UPST professionals.

"Did you see that?"

Chapter 15

I sat in Fayette Brown's room on the second floor of the Shelton Hotel amid a circle of investigators. I recognized the voice that had spoken as the eldest of the group sitting a person away to my right.

"I saw it," I responded, then added. "But don't say anything right now."

There was a chill in the room that was perceptible and I also sensed the group's angst. I had observed something in the next room that had obviously been seen by the lady near me. It turns out that she was a local person involved with the community and the youngsters knew her.

"The reason I asked you to say nothing," I continued, "is that I want you to write down a description of what you saw through the doorway and I'll do the same."

The young lady (who chose to remain anonymous) understood that I was verifying the experience. We didn't speak a word until we arrived back at the HQ.

Later, we both wrote down our experience and the following is an actual scan of our notes.

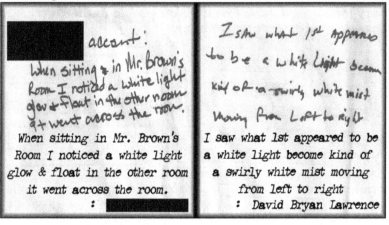

account: When sitting in Mr. Brown's Room I noticed a white light glow & float in the other room & it went across the room.	I saw what 1st appeared to be a white light become kind of a swirly white mist Moving from Left to right
When sitting in Mr. Brown's Room I noticed a white light glow & float in the other room it went across the room. :	I saw what 1st appeared to be a white light become kind of a swirly white mist moving from left to right : David Bryan Lawrence

***

222

FAYETTE III ACADEMY II

This year's Academy had bloomed to over one hundred and twenty people: Ninety-six on the beginners hunt, and twenty-six in the advanced (all night) crew. This was an incredible amount of students that I tried to break up with eight or ten for each of my squad leaders. Unfortunately, I got those leftover and on one walk-through I actually had 22 on my team. I ended up running them through the locations in five person shifts. It was not optimum but on the good side of it, I met a Grandmother with a crying and fearful child. I wondered "what is she

doing bringing a kid in a stroller?" On first glance, I realize this doesn't sound "good," but I later found the reason she was there is because she loves it! Her name is Linda Caron and she, her husband and son have all since been through the full academy and are considered among the elite of the UPST. All of my usual generals were at this academy including Christian, Robert, Allen Douglas, Mel, Jason and Bryson.

In the last couple of years, the UPST has captured some interesting evidence at the Superintendent's residence. This includes a responsive flashlight and a rolling tennis ball. I have mentioned the varied uses of flashlights before but for those of you that skip ahead, I will summarize. A flashlight if unscrewed to nearly the point of separation can still be triggered to turn on and off by movement or in our case paranormal activity. The theory is that a spirit in manifesting alters the Electro Magnetic Field (EMF) and can actually become a conductor if willing to trigger an electronic device, like a flashlight. In both of these instances at the Superintendent's house, the leads had been Melissa Olson and Jason Zupancic (nicknamed Zoop). I saw no need to challenge history and again appointed them to lead a rookie team to the Superintendent's House. These are two of my team that I especially trust to conduct a professional investigation while taking the time to teach. Interestingly enough, the teaching in this *swing* may have come at Jason's expense as you will see in the follow-up book the *UPST Case Study Digest*. In the last two years, Mel and Zoop had successfully captured evidence at the Superintendent's House. As I reminded Bryson of this history, I handed him an infrared camera.

"Come over here Bryson…," I took him aside. "Let Mel and Jason do they're thing… you know, like what they've been doing, but YOU keep this camera rolling every second you're in that house."

"Gotcha" Bryson acknowledged.

Melissa Olson and Jason Zupancic then took the team to the Superintendent's home with videographer and veteran UPST investigator Bryson Lawrence in tow. They found their way to the second floor main bedroom and began EVP work. This evening, in addition to the regular equipment they carried, Robert Declercq had slipped them a new piece of tech called an "obelisk."

"Apparently, you can use this box with the blinking lights to talk to us? Theoretically…" Zoop stated dubiously, "personally, I don't believe it."

The team sat in the empty room beneath the window of what once overlooked the total city and operation of Fayette and began an EVP/Obelisk session. To make this clearer I will put the "conversation" in the form of a play with the voice of the obelisk in brackets. This session took place in a time period of well over an hour in the superintendent's house. Interesting sections have been condensed and will be addressed in chronological order demonstrating the interaction that takes place in an investigation. This is as accurate as the transcript gets.

Jason (Zoop): Mr. Kitchen... are you here? (Zoop changes voice) old Clare gets all the attention... everybody likes a little dead girl.

[clarie]

Linda: Clare-e?

Zoop: Holy crap the box works.

[close]

Mel: Close?

[water]

Mel: Yes, we're close to the water.

[summer]

Linda: How old are you?

[twelve age]

Mel: Twelve age!

Jerri: Ian's twelve

Ian: Don't say that! (Ian, a youngster was not comfortable).

[teacher]

Mel: What's that?

Zoop: Sounded like teacher?

Linda: What's your name?

[zach]

Bryson: Zach

Linda: Zach, did you say Zach?

[did]

Linda: That's a nice name.

Jerri: That's a cool name Zach.

Chapter 15

Linda: Did you live in this house? This is a nice house. Twelve years old Zach…wow. Did you drown in the water? In the harbor?

[big… deep]

Jerri: Deep, oh …off a boat? Were you fishing?

Mel: You've got to give them a couple of seconds, if you ramble off questions they don't know which one to answer.

Zoop: do you wanta play hide and seek?

[do you have time]

Mel: Do you have time (Mel confirms)

Zoop: oh… sure… do you want to hide?

[sorry]

What you have just read is an interesting trail of questions and answers that seem to match up inferring intelligent response. It can be very exciting during a paranormal investigation, but in this case, it doesn't offer definitive proof that a Spirit (Frank's) Box or Obelisk is capable of spirit contact. What occurs in the continuation of this conversation and its potential as viable evidence will be addressed in the UPST's upcoming book on Case Studies. *CN: I remember that night we put up tents in the Shelton Hotel. I was in a tent with Robert and Allen and after my Dad fell asleep, the three of us heard a huge bang from upstairs. Later we heard it on the video camera with voices too.*

***

FAYETTE V

This was again a full investigation with experienced and accredited UPST Academy graduates, many who had gotten their first taste of paranormal investigation from a Fayette mini session a year or two before. In fact, many people have joined the UPST for several years in a row at

226

Fayette. This team includes: Linda and Tony Caron, Lisa and Jeff Miller with daughters Lindsay and Shania. Brenda, Craig and Audrey Raymond and other mainstays like Mel and Jason, Robert and Tony A., Christian and Investigators in Training like Al and Jenny Polequin were also present.

The night started out quite ordinarily with almost every squad eager to hit the Shelton other than Mel and Jason who had made their second paranormal home at the Superintendent's House. Tonight the Shelton would pay off in spades.

Christian's camera was illuminating the faces of our team every fifteen seconds and it was becoming irritating. Normally I ask for as many pictures as you can take, but the occasional snicker as my son viewed the LCD of the surprised person's expression had convinced me that he was enjoying it too much. I almost told him not to shoot people and that would have been a mistake as you will soon learn.

"Did anyone else see that?" I asked as we all sat in the familiar circular pattern in Fayette Brown's suite within the Shelton Hotel.

"I did." Audrey spoke sitting directly to my left.

I paused for a second and opted to break protocol as I had been here before and this was a bit different Audrey being an experienced investigator. As I related earlier, two years ago I had seen something in this room and had confirmed it, but now I wanted to chase it.

227

"What color?" I asked.

"Gray."

"To me it was black," I said and continued, "Was it moving?"

"Left to right," Audrey responded as though in a trance.

I noted the symmetry between our images and realized that I have a problem with visual colors. What I call brown is another's green and what is gray for another can be my black. We sat silently awaiting what might come next.

"THUD"

"What was that?" Al asked, standing near the wall, as he videoed the group of hunters sitting Indian style in the middle of the room. Christian continued his "in the face" photography as I decided what we would do. Since I'd also heard the load bang or thud from down the hall followed by what seemed to be footsteps, I decided to be proactive.

"Al," I spoke quietly, "you have the camera, come with me and we'll check it out." The team continued to sit quietly as we exited the room to track down the sound alone. We ran through several reenactments in an attempt to duplicate the footsteps. Again, I decide to break protocol by leaving an IIT out on his own, but with a reason. He was the only investigator standing and I didn't want to disturb the ambience of the atmosphere that we had established within the room. I asked that Al again try to duplicate the steps we had experienced earlier and I requested complete silence as Al made his sweep.

"My neck is so sore," Brenda sighed, "I feel like something is pushing down on me."

"Me too," Audrey concurred.

Christian racked off several photos of the two ladies in distress as we sat in the dark. Brenda had been having health problems but the last thing I had expected to hear was about her neck. After nearly three minutes and countless Christian snapshots, we all heard the thud again.

"Ho…hoh hoah," Al had broken his own silence and then exhaled uncomfortably. "DAVE, Dave…. Dave."

Although his voice had been low and controlled I had heard it and sensed an urgency that required immediate attention. The video tape reveals Al breathing heavily at this point. I handed my equipment to Audrey on my left and stood up to go to into the dark Shelton hallway. Peering out into the long corridor I faintly saw Al's infrared LED about forty feet from me. I walked his way as he moved toward me meeting at the top of the main staircase. I felt a sudden chill.

"Al, you can come back," I said.

"Holy *********** sake," Al interjected.

I could now see Al at the top of the stairway. I asked "what happened?"

"I …could, just froze down there."

"What, you mean you just got the chills?"

"I mean like chills, goose bumps, everything," Al replied. At this point on the video you can hear a vibration that had initially confused me until Al said:

"Look, my hand is shaking."

Chapter 15

I had seen this in the Shelton before and I actually feared that Al might pass out, so I opted to give him a break with the team in Fayette's room after a short re-focus on debunking. He seemed up to the task, so we tried to recreate the footsteps as he videotaped me. After several takes I asked Al if he were still uncomfortable or could he join me longer in the corridor.

"Nope, I'm fine."

We did find a door down a nearby exit that may have been the thud that we had heard and closed it firmly so that the next team in didn't have to contend with it.

"Yeah, whatever it is, it's here."

Craig Raymond spoke as he came out into the hallway to alert me to Brenda's further distress and was standing near the top of the staircase where Al and I had been moments ago. "I can still feel it."

"What do you mean?" I asked.

"I mean, it's right here...it's cold right here," Craig murmured as he leaned on the rail of at the top of the stairway. "I don't feel good here."

We all returned to the Brown room but I could tell that Craig was feeling uneasy at the top of the stairs near where Al had his incident. We all knew something was here. In the meantime, Christian was continuing his random photography of the team as Craig. Al and I re-entered Fayette Brown's room. The team members had continued their EVP work through our absence, and were now drained.

"Let's swing it," I said.

***

The night had gotten chilly as Lisa and Jeff Miller's squad finished their swing in the Hotel. Robert Declercq and Tony A., along with Linda, Tony and Jaime Caron were about ready to start their own shift in the haunted Shelton. Melissa and Jason's squad were still out at the Superintendent's house.

"Anything happen to you guys over there?" Robert probed our team for information.

I jumped in immediately. "No, no," I directed my team, "Don't say anything right now… Robert, I would rather you go in blind not knowing what or where, ok?"

"Gotcha," Robert concurred as he grabbed his camera from the table top where it had been charging. He looked toward the Caron family. "You three ready?"

"As ready as I'll ever be," Linda made the *brrrrr* shake signal as she spoke.

"Hey David, be sure to check out that picture Lisa took," Robert shot off as he walked out the door.

"I will," I replied.

As Robert and his crew headed across the road, the remainder of our team stood going over photographic evidence in the Jackson Iron Company office where we had laid out our headquarters. I turned toward the small circle of my team trying to stay warm.

"David," Brenda called me over to where she sat, "Show your Dad, Christian."

Christian sidled up to me and replayed through the long string of photos he had taken in the Shelton. What I saw was close-up pictures of my team as we sat on the floor of Fayette Brown's suite.

"Ok, and what am I seeing?"

"Look at this picture," Christian said holding the camera viewer to my eyes, "and now this one."

Chapter 15

I looked closer at what appeared to be a black cloud around Brenda's head. Christian shuffled ahead to the next photo which was also of Brenda. This time there was no shadow. *CN: I knew I had something here... it was just too weird to see like 10 shots in a row and the differences when she was saying her neck hurt.*

Brenda chirped in with her Oklahoma drawl, "David that is exactly when my neck was hurting so much... did you hear me say that?"

"Yeah," I recalled and slapped Christian on the back, "nice catch son."

In reflection, this is an unusual anomaly mainly because the photos taken surrounding it are unmarred. It immediately put me in mind of a Thai horror film later remade in Japan and the United States called *Shutter*. If you haven't seen this flick, check it out and you'll get an idea of the creep factor that this photo can give you. But the best was yet to come.

"Give me a minute and I'll find that picture, David,"

Lisa Miller had taken me aside and was rifling through her randomly snapped catalogue of the earlier Fayette hunt. I should point out that Lisa is our best hope for a world-class photographer as she seems to have a knack for catching something odd on every hunt. This night would be no exception.

"Where is it from?"

"Second story of the Shelton by the top of the stairs," Lisa responded.

"You have got to be kidding!?" I thought.

But after what we had already experienced at the Shelton Hotel, nothing else would be surprising me tonight. What Lisa showed me was the clear black outline of what appeared to be a man standing very near the spot where Al and Craig had their personal experiences.

Shelton Hotel: 3 ms before and after

` "Who is it?" I asked.

"That's just it," Lisa exhaled, "its no one… none of us were standing there."

***

FAYETTE V ACADEMY

III

I wanted to include a simple outside hunt in this book, so I chose the aged fisherman's cemetery of Fayette. *CN: One of my favorite locations because something always happens.* It sits not quite two miles from the town site and in the past we have walked that distance even in the pouring rain to visit this gem of Fayette history.

When doing any outside location bring all of the necessities. This includes umbrellas, food and drinks and lots of extra batteries. Many times, as I have written earlier, we bring along a Coleman lantern to use as a central marker and for hand warmth if we need it. Although we have been to this particular cemetery more than once, I just wanted to touch on some points that make an outdoor hunt great.

Chapter 15

First of all, in a small cemetery one of the bonuses is that we are usually within sight and sound of each other. This has led to the capture of evidence in many cases when one person has a personal experience and the other the equipment. *CN: We didn't hit the cemetery the first couple of years, but now I think it is the perfect way to end a hunt.* Of course, proximity is not the rule in many modern

cemeteries but the Fayette location is about one hundred and fifty years old and served a small nearby community. Second, the history of such a location is actually palpable. Standing in front of a thirty year old man who died in 1877 can bring imagination into a melding with reality. Did this man die in a fishing accident or of tuberculosis? Did he fight in the Civil War as a teenager? How about the mother and the child that died on the same day in 1894? Empathy and conjecture can run rampant while EVP questioning can grow from the team's perception of these clues.

One of the conditions of these old graveyards is that most have outlived their relatives. In other words, there is little or no upkeep by survivors. Cemeteries like the Trudell near Rock River, Michigan are few and far between. This is a graveyard that is still kept up by some unknown descendent and is off the beaten track in the middle of the woods. It is very difficult to locate. There are only three graves on site for sisters who died in 1925 from Black Tongue Diphtheria. Visiting this spot is mystical and moving. The Fayette Fisherman's Cemetery is similar in all

but that it is not kept up. This is where my team comes in. In the past, we have actually organized UPST picnics at these sites and cared for the graves. We are planning one at the Fisherman's Cemetery in the near future. In most cases, we do onsite repair. On this night, Al Polequin, another man taking part in our Fayette mini academy and myself lifted several monuments back into place. My back can attest to the fact that one of these headstones weighed nearly five hundred pounds. It is a good thing that Al and I are big guys.

The Upper Peninsula Spook Team members have created a reputation as the good guys and the authorities recognize this. More than once we have been told by local officials that they favor our frequenting a location rather than the usual drunken teenagers. They can actually count on us to police the site when they cannot. Whether it is a huge graveyard or Fayette, solemnity and respect for the dead are primary attributes that all paranormal teams should embrace. As you have read in the previous chapters, my son Christian has been re-planting the flags of our fallen since he began hunting graveyards at four years old. This is something I require from my team and something that you should expect from your own.

"Yeah," Christian said,
"Why don't you get that one over there Gabe."
Christian directed his cousin Gabriel to replant
a fallen flag on a veteran's grave. He had been leading his cousins
Rylie, Teagan and Gabe along with family friend Jacob through
the cemetery on a UPST junior hunt.
I had conducted some business downtown and came
back to the cemetery where I'd watched from a distance, taking
pride in the little troop of investigators maintaining
the cemetery graves. I joined the group.
"Now, look here," I said to the youngsters, *"you can tell that this lady
probably died in childbirth by the dates on her grave and the child
next to her."*
We walked through the multitude of grave markers dating from
the late 19th century to present. There is much to be learned
from the dates, names and titles like Mother or Father
that adorn these stones.

-Manistique Lakeview Cemetery, 9:45 PM

16

The Final Word

I thank you for reading this book and further hope that you now have the tools to start your own family team. Paranormal investigation is a pastime worthy of comparison to a family softball team with a bit more reading, and actually, after a three day investigation you will feel like you have run a marathon. This is part of the game that is addictive... sometimes you don't know where you get the energy from, but it keeps coming, especially when you have to keep up with your kids.

Please stay tuned with the UPST for the upcoming **UPST Case Study Digest** which will add at least ten more adventures and in depth updates of the cases you have read already. Past locations in addition to the Upper Peninsula and Michigan will be reviewed from Illinois, Ohio, Florida, California, Wisconsin, W. Virginia, New Jersey, Mexico, Canada, Haiti, etc.

Also, be sure to sign up for the UPST Update Newsletter. Opportunities to enroll in the UPST Academy, merchandise specials, and morsels of upcoming books are given to you just for signing up! Send your email to davidbryanlawrence@hotmail.com or just sign up at the UPST website at www.upspookteam.info.

The following appendixes show forms that can be duplicated by your team for use in your upcoming investigation. For instance, with the ghost traps and the grid, just lay the book on a copy machine and simply expand them, add your team name and information and off you go. The Glossarex is a combination of a Glossary with an Index featuring relevant terms and a listing of UPST certified investigators.

In finishing this book, I again thank my UPST family, who without, Ghost Hunting would be a whole lot lonelier ☺

David Bryan Lawrence

UPST

_____ INVESTIGATION LOG SHEET Date: _____

Location & History note: _____

Members Present: _____

_____

_____

Temperature: _____

Humidity: _____

Moon: _____

Barometric Pressure:____

Equipment used:

Still cameras:_____

Video Cameras: _____

type:_____

type:_____

type:_____

type:_____

EMF Meter:

type:_____

Audio recorder:

type:_____

Thermometer:

type:_____

type:_____

type:_____

Other:

Area code_____

(_____)

Time In: _____

Time Out: _____

ADDITIONAL COMMENTS

ADDITIONAL COMMENTS

Ambient room temperature: _____ EMF Baseline:_____

Events/Meter changes: _____

_____

_____

_____

_____

_____

239

Appendix I Investigator Log

_____ **INVESTIGATOR LOG SHEET   Date:** _____

Location and squad: _____

NAME_____

Area _____ Time In:_____ Time Out: _____

Ambient room temperature: _____ EMF Baseline: _____

Events/Meter changes:_____

_____

_____

_____

_____

Area_____ Time In: _____Time Out _____

Ambient room temperature: _____ EMF Baseline: _____

Events/Meter changes: _____

_____

_____

_____

Area_____ Time In: _____Time Out _____

Ambient room temperature: _____ EMF Baseline: _____

Events/Meter changes:_____

_____

_____

_____

ADDITIONAL COMMENTS

240

INVESTIGATION GRID Location: _____ Date: _____

Hot Spot	Session 1	Session 2	Session 3	Session 4	Session 5	Session 6
Area 1						
Area 2						
Area 3						
Area 4						
Area 5						
Area 6						

Appendix II Grid Sample

UPST INVESTIGATION GRID Location: MARQUETTE Date: 4/6/12

Hot Spot	Session 1	Session 2	Session 3	Session 4	Session 5	Session 6
Child's Bedroom	ICPI – MEL & JASON	CRISTIAN & ROBERT	DAVID & BRYSON	X	X	AUDREY & DAVID
Area 1 Kitchen	X	ICPI	X	X	X	Christian ← Bryson
Area 2 Living Room	CRAIG – AUDREY – BRENDA	Bryson Monitor	Christian & ZOOP	Roberto – Brys & C-MAN	BRENDA Monitor	X
Area 3 Basement	DAVID & ROBERT	X	X	ICPI Jas & Mel	Christian Brys & Audrey	X
Area 4 MASTER BR UPSTAIRS	Christian & Brys	DAVID – CRAIG – AND & BRENDA	CRAIG, AUD, BRENDA	CRAIG	ICPI & Robert	CRAIG – Rob & BRENDA
Area 5 Upstairs BR 2	X	X	Roberto & Mel	Audrey & BRENDA	X	ICPI
Area 6 CLOSET / OUTSIDE	X	X	X	DAVID Lockdown	CRAIG & DAVID OUTSIDE BREAK	2:35 ICPI OUT

UPST Bulls-Eye Ghost Trap

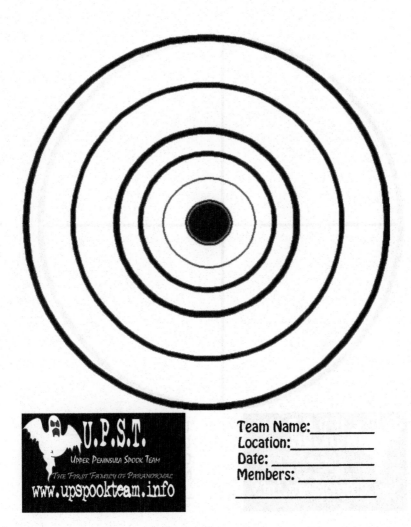

Team Name:_____
Location:_____
Date: _____
Members: _____
_____

UPST Cross-Hair Ghost Trap

Team Name:_____
Location:_____
Date: _____
Members: _____
_____

Glosserex (Glossary AND Index)
Chapters = C
Photos = P

Abductee: In the field of the paranormal, an abductee is someone taken against their will by a nonhuman. Another term is experiencer. This word is considered an alternative to "abductee," being less negative.

ABSM: An ABSM is any of a variety of reported hairy bipeds from around the world. Though the term is derived from Abominable Snowman, it is considered a less sensational alternative to Sasquatch, Bigfoot, Yeti, Stink Ape, Liberal, etc.

Adas, Anthony: (Tony) UPST Certified Investigator. C15

Afterlife: Life after death. The word "afterlife" has been in use since 1615. See also: Cross Over and "the other side." 3, 4, 35, 215.

Agent: A person who is the focus of poltergeist or personally oriented activity.

Agriglyph: Or Crop Circle is a large design created in a field of vegetation by pressing down parts of the growth. Some believe it is extraterrestrial.

Aliens: Visitors from other planets. We differentiate aliens from visitors that may live in parallel worlds, the otherworld, or what's commonly called the afterlife.

Altered State of Consciousness: A mental state that is different from a normal waking state. The term created by Charles Tart describes changes in the mental condition. A similar phrase used is "altered state of awareness."

Amulet: An object that is thought to bring good luck or have the power to protect from ghosts or spirits and ward off evil.

Analysis: Post investigation, the team will go over all media and evidence collected for anomalies. 17, 24, 34, 61, 74-76, 85, 91, 108-110, 146, 160, 217.

Anemometer: Used for meteorological measurement this device detects wind and its velocity. Spontaneous drafts of air can be measured with this tool. See also: Wind Meter. 96.

Angels: Angels are supernatural entities found in many religions. In Christianity, Judaism and Islam they typically act as messengers. 10, 14. See Also: Guardian Angel, Inhuman Entity, and Satan.

Anniversary Imprint: A haunting that usually manifests around the same time each year. See Residual Spirit.

Appendix IV Glossarex

Anomaly: Something out of the ordinary or unexplainable. In paranormal, referring to any phenomenon that cannot be debunked. 109, 164, 232.

Apocalypse: Is a term most often applied to the end of the world, the dawn of a new world or the revelation before mankind's final judgment.

Apparition: An apparition is an appearance to the living of a ghost, usually taking the form of a visual image of a deceased individual. 12, 16, 18, 61, 98, 125, 157, 174, 193.

Apport: Objects that materialize or appear at will in the presence of a medium.

Ararat Anomaly: The Ararat Anomaly is a large object (over 90 meters in length) photographed on Mount Ararat in Turkey. Some people believe it is Noah's Ark.

Arkeology: The search for the physical remains of Noah's Ark.

Asport: A physical object that spirit's teleport to another location or make disappear.

Astral body: Refers to the mental personage which exists alongside the physical body. This becomes the being that a person occupies during an out-of-body experience.

Astral plane: A plane of existence that is viewed as enlightened and desirable according to some religion and philosophies. Believed to be beyond and above the "normal" world.

Astral Projection: The experience of one's spirit leaving the body and enter the astral plane. Also called "out of body experience."

Astral: Relating to a subtle body and plane of existence that coexist with and survive the death of the human physical body.

Astrology: The theory that positions of celestial bodies have influence over natural earthly occurrences and human affairs.

Audio Recorder: Makes re-playable records of sounds on tape (analog) or digitally (digital). 75, 122, 217.

Aura: Energy field or life force surrounding all, objects within our realm.

Automatic Writing: (Autoism) An unconscious or involuntary muscular movement caused by spirits where a subject blindly writes whatever comes to mind.

Autoscopy: The image of one's mental embodiment looking back at themselves from a position outside the body. See also: Out of Body Experience.

AVP: Audible Voice Phenomena are unnatural sounds or voices that can be heard in real time and recorded, whereas EVP is usually captured in review of the audio. See also: EVP.

Background: The team researcher's primary duty is to gather pre-hunt information about the location, history, clients and their experiences. This research becomes the "background" for the case, often adding additional texture to the EVP sessions.

Ball Lightning: A rare phenomena in the shape of a glowing red ball lasting between a few seconds to several minutes. Associated with thunderstorms, these spheres are thought to consist of ionized gas and can affect readings on para-electric tools.

Banshee: Based in Irish lore. A "wailing spirit" often appearing as an omen of death.

Barometer: Gauge that measures barometric pressure. 66.

Baseline: An established pre-hunt normal measurement of temperature, radiation, electro magnetic fields, etc. to aid in the noting of anomalies during an investigation. 24, 49, 89, C10-15, P239, P240. See also: Primary Readings.

Belanger, Tania: UPST Certified Investigator and Upper Peninsula MUFON (Midwest Unidentified Flying Object Network) agent. 68, 272, C11, P160, P162.

Bennett, Lori: Early UPST member retired. C13, C15, P182, P188, P211, P271.

Black Mass: Usually considered a negative manifestation of an entity. 18, 140, 148, 168, 228,233. See also: Shadow Ghost.

Blue: Robert Declercq's dog often used in paranormal investigation before his passing.

Bolide: An exploding meteor resembling a bright fireball. Can cause electronic or magnetic anomalies.

Bongo: A past or random UPST member dismissed due to the incomprehension of team and/or family values. VIII, 114.

Camera: A device that takes photographs. Even in these years if it isn't digital, a 35mm SLR still has a place in investigation. 73.

Cameron, Sara: UPST member and the granddaughter of Betty Lustila and cousin of the family Lawrence. C15, P27, P28.

Capone, Alphonse: ("Al", "Scarface") 1899-1947. Italian born gangster, murderer & bootlegger out of Chicago. C11.

Caron, Jaime: UPST Certified Investigator and actor in residence. 26, 223, 231, P26.

Appendix IV Glossarex

Caron, Linda: UPST Certified Investigator, cook and movie star. 26,121, C14, C15, P1, P7, P113, P121, P238.

Caron, Tony: UPST Certified Investigator, diver and sailor. C14, C15, P7, P238.

Case Study: An in-depth investigation of an individual subject or location. 17, 53, 63, C10-15, 237, 271.

Case: An investigation request that has been accepted after which the team leader will organize the pre-hunt, assign the researcher and designate team members to their tasks, set up and complete the investigation.

Chakra: An aspect of consciousness associated with multiple physiological functions.

Channeling: Process of receiving and transmitting messages or information from spirits.

Chrono-Trigger: (chronology-trigger) An item, sound, smell, etc. that appeals to the time period or targeted spirit. 131, 186, 187.

Chupacabra: Primarily reported in southern realms of the Americas, a beast that feeds on livestock. Possibly a relative of the Michigan Dog Man.

Clairaudience: An auditory form of ESP paranormal information received outside the range of normal perception through voices, whispers, physical sensations or smells.

Cleaning: Sometimes called "clearing." The practice of ushering a malignant energy to "cross over" or to leave a haunted location.

Clearing: Ridding a location of ghostly activity.

Cold Reading: A system commonly used by fake psychics and mediums which allows them to obtain information about a person by asking a universal sequence of questions. Sociopaths accomplish this effortlessly picking up on expression, mood and reaction.

Cold Spots: Sometimes called the "chills." A sudden temperature drop that is believed the energy drain associated with a sprit's attempted manifestation. 17-19, 24, 65, 80, 96-98, 147, 184.

Collective Apparition: When different persons witness an incident independently or simultaneously. Only one in ten apparition sightings fall into this category. C15.

Compass: Points out direction based on the magnetic North and can also be used as a makeshift EMF detector. 63.

Control Group: A group of subjects whose normal performance or abilities are compared with experimental subjects.

Control: Standard set of operation that insures an experiment is conducted within an unbiased and objective parameter. For instance: All teams have an Infrared Camera.

Crisis Apparition: A vision seen when a person is ill, injured or at the point of death.

Crone: Also termed the "Old Hag Syndrome. A dream state oppression that involves a feeling of immobilization and suffocation, often including waking to find an old woman on your chest. With Scandinavian or Slavic origins now reported worldwide. See also: Old Hag Syndrome.

Cross Over: The act believed what most living entities carry out upon death when entering the afterlife.

Crypto zoology: The study of animals or legends considered mythical or extinct. These include Sasquatch (Big Foot), the Loch Ness Monster and the Chupacabra.

Debunk: The UPST considers this the art of the hunt. Debunking is deducing logical explanations for existent phenomena. All "activity" we debunk leaves us more time for the actual investigation. 49, 61, 63, 97, 126, 140, 141, 149, 182, 184, 230.

Declercq, Robert: UPST Certified Investigator and head of UPST affiliate Spirit Chasers. The master of weird equipment and one of the UPST Generals. 26, 121, 168, 190, C14, C15, P107, P115, P121, P168, P190, P193, P209, P212, P214.

Déjà vu: The feeling that you have experienced a scenario or a happening before.

Dé KlunK: The act of one who has difficulty with schedules and or an inability to make their own plans clear.

Dematerialization: The fading of a spirit or apparition into the otherworld.

Demon: (or daemon) Most religions say a demon is representative of evil or Satan. 10-15.

Demonology: The study of demons or beliefs about demons and the practice and resources to fight them. 10-15.

Determinations: The summary or conclusion of the investigation. The UPST grades a hunt based on historical value, precedence and activity.

Devil: (Satan) The supreme leader of evil believed to command lower entities called demons. 182.

Digital Camera: This invention has revolutionized ghost hunting with unlimited capability to take photos and see them without the time of development. 59.

Digital Thermometer: Detects ambient room temperature , contrary to infrared thermometers that measure surface temperature. 65.

Dillinger, John: 1902-34. Gangster, bank robber & murderer. C11.

Disembodied Voice: An unexplainable voice that can be AVP or EVP. 4, 22, 85.

Dobson, Danielle: UPST Certified Investigator, member of UPST affiliate ICPI (Iron County Paranormal Investigation) and Niece of Melissa Olson. C14. P199, P201,

Doppelganger: A figure or apparition of a person appearing identical to the living but behaving independently.

Douglas, Allen: UPST member & Spirit Chaser alumni. C15, P223.

Dowsing: Using the movement of metal rods, sticks, pendulums, etc. to obtain information (also called divining). 64, 65, 86, 172, 174. See also: EMF (Electro Magnetic Field).

Dream Communication: Usually occurring before or in early REM state where one has a dream of persons or incidents past or future of which they are not previously aware.

Dust: Often mistaken for "orbs" in photographs. 21, 61, 147.

DVR: Digital Video Recorder. Used in surveillance systems and other video devices. 90, 91, P87.

Earthbound: A spirit unable to crossover at the time of death that may be confused or without option to do so.

Ectoplasm: A substance exuded by ghosts and sometimes by mediums communicating with the spirit world and usually photographed as a cloudy vaporous mist but also thought can be gelatinous. 18, 19, 108.

Eisenberger, Ed and Suzell: Owners of the House of Ludington, gracious hosts and excellent chefs. C11.

Electrical Strip: A multi-port electrical supply for 120V. 97.

Electro magnetic Energy: A combination of electrical and magnetic fields inherent in and around electrical systems or anomalies. See also: EMF.

Elemental: Spirits drawing on one of the four elements: earth, wind, water or fire. Some believe they manifest as nature spirits that include faeries, trolls and banshees.

EMF - Electro Magnetic Field Detector: A tool detecting a combination of electrical and magnetic fields theorized generated by a spirit when manifesting. 24, 56, 76-78, 92, 93, 96, C10-15.

Empath: Senses and feels the emotions of others. (From empathize).

Entity An entity is something that has a distinct, separate existence. See also: Chapter 2.

Environmental Data: Environmental conditions can impede an investigation in every area from clothing to equipment malfunction. Be aware of the weather, geophysical and other issues that will affect your investigation.

Epicenter: Person or location that a haunting surrounds and activity increases.

ESP - Extrasensory perception: Communication or understanding by means other than the physical senses. Most humans have this ability, although typically dormant.

Evidence: Anomalies that cannot be debunked. Whether audio, video, temperature, etc. any incident catalogued and unexplainable by standard means.

Evil Spirit: Either a human or non-human entity that may be inherent or summoned. Two methods of beckoning made trendy in film are Ouija boards or through satanic worship. See also: Demon.

Evil: In religion and ethics, evil refers to the morally or ethically objectionable behavior or thought that is hateful, cruel, excessively violent, and devoid of conscience.

EVP: Or Electronic voice phenomena is the disembodied voice or sound emitted by a spirit spontaneously, repetitiously or when questioned. Usually discovered post-hunt and recorded on electronic devices. 22-24, 75-76, 88, 91.

Exorcism: Evicting demons or other evil entities from a person or a location by using religious rites. See also: Possession.

Explained: Debunking activity with ordinary evidence. If this occurs at a location, it means that a follow up will not be necessary.

Extra Sensory Perception: Also known as ESP. Communication or perception by means other than the physical senses.

Extraterrestrial: A being from out of our realm; from outer space or out of our galaxy.

Eye In The Sky: Multiple satellites used for surveillance of life and movement on the planet earth; from your doorway to your car. Skeptics See Also: GPS

Appendix IV Glossarex

Eyewitness: A direct observer to an event. In paranormal, this person experiences an activity in the first person and relates it.

Eyewitness Testimony: The UPST advocates speaking to and interviewing eyewitness but realizes that this is often the most unreliable of evidence. Even a trained investigator's eyewitness testimony without documentation (multiple witness, recording, etc.) is not a reliable form of evidence in an investigation.

Faeries: This refers to a small being that lives parallel to our world or not far from it. Many people who readily accept the reality of ghosts don't believe in faeries. Some people use sprite and fairy interchangeably. See also: Sprite.

False Awakening: Sometimes called a "false waking." The event in which a person believes they are awake but are actually dreaming.

Faraday Cage: Comes from the name of physicist Michael Faraday, who in 1836 invented the Faraday cage, also known as a "Faraday shield." Used in the paranormal it insulates EMF and other activity from whatever is inside. See also: EMF.

Faustus, Doctor Johann: Physician and alchemist was the inspiration for the plays by Goethe and Marlow about a deal with the devil. See also: Obama.

Fayette: A Federal and State historical park. In the late 1800's a thriving community now open to tourists. Once known as Fayette Ghost town due to its near desertion. An active paranormal locale. 84, C15, P4, P7, P13, P20, P22, P29, P31, P34, P106, P107, P274.

Fear Cage: Homage to the Faraday Cage although very different. A fear cage is an area inside a building that has unusually high EMFs usually because of faulty wiring. Effects on human beings include paranoia, oppression, sensations of being watched, etc.

Fetch: A phantom twin of a living person. See also: Doppelganger and Wraith.

Fetish: Aside from the modern sexual connotation, a fetish is the tool of a shaman usually a pouch that has magical items or a figurine with similar qualities.

Fischer, Marilyn: Noted historian, author and paranormal expert. Also heads the Gulliver Historical Society that preserves and manages the Seul Choix Pointe Lighthouse. C10.

Flapper: 1.A piece of cardboard or cloth taped to the top of a static camera in a lavatory to allow privacy when needed. 2. A 1920's party girl. 160.

Floating Orb: Spherical glowing ball picked up on video and photographs. Most times an orb is white but at times may have different colors. 21. See also: Orb.

Floor Plans: Usually used to locate equipment and squads to avoid cross talk and false evidence..

Footsteps: Sometimes called footfalls, are a common feature of many investigations. One of the primary points attacked by skeptics with reasoning from mass hallucination to matrixing. Fortunately, audio recordings don't lie. See also: Matrixing and Pareidolia.

Frank's Box: Sometimes referred to as a Ghost Box or Spirit Box, Frank's Box was invented by Frank Sumpton. It scans AM/FM frequencies non-stop under the theory that spirit voices can communicate in real time. 88.

Fried, Sara: UPST Certified Investigator & photographer. C14, P82.

Gas Detector: Usually detects combustible gases. Some of these can be important to hunts (Paulding Light) and others to symptoms of oppression (Fayette Methane). 89, P89.

Geiger Counter: There are different types of Geiger Counters, but basically they all detect gamma radiation. The theory is that when an entity manifests itself there may be an emission of radiation. P89.

Gehn, Edward: (Ed) Serial killer made infamous by books and movies like: Psycho, Silence of the Lambs, and the Texas Chainsaw Massacre. Jeffrey Dahmer influence. Visited at Plainfield, WI. Cemetery by Christian and David. P8.

Ghost: Usually refers to the manifestation of the spirit or soul of a dead human (or animal) that exists in different forms on an earthly plane. 10, C2. See also: Cross Over.

Ghost Box: A device used for contacting spirits through the use of radio frequency scanning. This method is thought to provide "real time" communication and subsequent recording. 88-89. See also: Frank's box, Spirit Box.

Ghost Hunter: A person who investigates locales in search of paranormal activity. There are three different types of ghost hunters. The UPST makes use of two of them; those who practice the scientific method and the occasional psychic or medium. We chose not to work with the third type whom refuse to carry equipment that documents evidence; whether psychic or newbie.

Appendix IV Glossarex

Ghost Hunting: The practice of investigating an alleged haunting or occasionally a locale when summoned to aid a family or person in distress. The UPST investigates using the scientific method as they observe and record data with electronic tools. Gadgets include EMF Meters, digital thermometers, infrared night vision cameras, handheld video cameras, digital audio recorders, and computers.

Ghost Lights: These are mysterious lights, seen at a distance, usually appearing as blue or yellow spheres, which can appear to blink. This phenomenon has been sighted all over the world and in many cultures. See also: Paulding Light, Vortex, and Portal.

Ghost Phone: Thomas Edison was the son of two spiritualists in Canada and was working on this project when he died. The plans are considered lost.

Ghost Trap: A paranormal tool produced by the UPST and employed through the use of cross-hair and bulls-eye diagrams that precisely measure kinetic movement. Often used with a chrono-trigger. 60-61, 82, 131-149. P61, P82, P181, P185. See: Chrono-trigger.

Ghoul: A nocturnal grave robber. Sometimes a living thief but is also represented in art and horror as an ugly, flesh-eating fiend.

Giles, Rob: UPST Certified Investigator, computer expert and noted skeptic. 86, C14-15, P41, P55, P184, P186, P188, P271.

Gisslander, Mary: UPST member & Spirit Chaser alumni known for EVP recording expertise.190, C15, P7, P101,P113 P107, P190, P217.

Glow Rods: Inexpensive glow in the dark sticks, necklaces, etc. Made with luminescent phosphorus chemicals. 66.

God: The name refers to the deity held by monotheists to be the Supreme Being. God is regarded as the sole creator of the universe.

GPS: (Global Positioning System) Used to locate a transmission on a map of the earth. Only three (tri-location) are necessary but now the system works in double digits. 90.

Grey: Also called a Gray is an alien category that evolved from a reported 1947 UFO crash and description of two alien creatures recovered in Roswell, New Mexico.

Grid: A written schedule of rooms and or buildings that compile an investigation. Used for team rotation and the knowledge of their location. 105, 193, 208, 216, 219, P219, P241, P242.

Guardian Angel: A spirit who is assigned to protect and guide a particular person. Often encountered in NDE. See also: Near Death Experience, Out of Body Experience.

Hallucination: False or distorted perception of sights and sounds appearing to be real.

Harbinger: A spirit of the future that warns of things to come. E.g. "beware the harbinger of doom," E.g. Letters or kind words from ex-wives or from the Friend of the Court.

Haunting: Any recurring activity or phenomena linked to intelligent or residual entities. A pattern of paranormal activity at a specific location leads it to be classified as haunted.

Hazlett, Lindsay: UPST Certified Investigator and member of the Jeff and Lisa Miller family. 227. P99, P238.

Heat Lightning: Created through convergent pressure zones and static electricity. Can cause havoc with paranormal gear.

Heaven: A plane of existence in religions that is considered the apex of the afterlife.

Hell: Many religions regard this as an afterlife of suffering where a sinner is punished for all eternity. Often imagined as fiery and always with the absence of God.

Hellhound: A spectral death omen in the form of a ghostly dog. See also: Harbinger.

Helmer House Inn: Finished in 1881, this beautiful Michigan historical landmark is located in Helmer, MI. and has an abundance of paranormal activity. 6, 87, 97, 100, 273, C12.

Hoax: A staged occurrence meant to fool for attention or financial gain. The UPST takes pride in debunking and duplicating contrived "evidence."

Hot Reading: Yet another trick used by fake mediums where they are given prior knowledge of their subject.

Hot Spot: The place within a haunted location where the activity is most prevalent.

Houdini, Harry: Born Eric Weiss in Appleton, Wisconsin in 1874. An escapologist and magician who made his life task the debunking of spiritualism. Having an open mind, he left his wife secret words to be delivered upon his death from the afterlife. Houdini died in Michigan in 1926 never delivering his message. 4.

House of Ludington: Built in 1865 and a Michigan historical landmark located in Escanaba, MI. Rumored to be a favorite of Al Capone and Baby Face Nelson. Fantastic experience and good food. 6, 68, 104,135, 273, C11, P68.

Appendix IV Glossarex

Hypnagogia: Is what a person can experience in the hypnagogic state, the period of falling asleep. These can be anything from lucid dreams and sleep paralysis to psychic prediction.

Hypnosis: Induced condition of an altered state of consciousness where the subject acts only on external suggestion.

Hypnotherapy: When hypnosis is used as therapy due to the extreme suggestibility of the subject. Fears and habits have been alleviated through the use of hypnotherapy.

Ignis fatuus: A glowing or supernatural light that is alleged to be indicative of death. Some believe it is combustion of gases from decomposing organic materials.

IIT: Investigator in Training. 45, 47, 48, 97, 228. See also: Newbie.

Illusion: A false observation between what is real and what is seen.

Imprint: Activity that appears unthinking and redundant. See also: Residual Spirit.

Incarnation: A bodily manifestation of a supernatural being, usually into a human body.

Inconclusive: Evidence has been gathered but analysis is disputed amongst the investigators. Thus a conclusion is not merited.

Incorporeal: From the Latin for "lacking material form or substance."

Infrared: (Used interchangeably with video camera). Also known as IR. Digital video, some cameras and other tools used by the UPST are equipped with the capability to penetrate darkness by illuminating the infrared light spectrum. Shadows have become an issue of contention as some investigators believe that shadows are illuminated by infrared when in fact it is the opposite; more shadows are seen without. 82-84, 90-94, C7. P82.

Infrared Thermometer: Infrared thermometers measure the temperature of a surface remotely. 78-79, P78.

Inhuman Entity: A supernatural being that didn't begin existence in human form, such as: demons, angels, elementals, jinn, etc.

Intelligent Haunting: Activity resulting from a spirit is labeled intelligent if it has the ability to interact with human beings. 12-16.

Intuition: Any knowledge gained through a perceptive insight. 48.

Intuitive: A person sensitive to any knowledge perceived from other than direct experience such as feelings of enlightenment or fear.

Ion: An electrically charged atom or molecule.

Jinn: Genie is the English term for the Jinn, a race of supernatural creatures from Islamic and Arabian mythos.

Johnson, Kayla: UPST Certified Investigator and member of affiliate ICPI (Iron County Paranormal Investigation). Currently in the Western United States. C15.

Jolly Inn: Located in Germfask, MI. This facility is a classic Upper Peninsula delight: Good food, good atmosphere and good paranormal activity. 6, 61, 169, 273, C13, P104,

Jungian: Analytical psychology founded by Carl Jung often invoked by experts on the paranormal because Jung thought of the human psyche as inherently mystical.

K2 Meter: Or a KII meter monitors energy fields that spirits disrupt when near. It contains five L.E.D. lights that increase as the EMFs strength grows. See also: EMF. 64, 92-93.

Kaluza, Jacob: UPST Certified Investigator and friend of Christian, Teagan and Gabe Lawrence on UPST Juniors. 236, P38, P39, P50, P110, P236.

Karma: Believed to be a sum of all that an individual has done, is currently doing, will do and how these actions will affect his fate. Further: the belief that a negative or generous act receives like.

Kin, Wendy Jo: UPST Certified Investigator. 82, C14.

Kinetic: Movement of objects. See also: Ghost Trap, Psychokinesis, and Telekinesis. 12, 14, 24, 61, 83, 128, 180, 192.

Kirlian photography: Created by Semyon Kirlian in 1939 accidently. It creates corona discharge on the contact print of a photograph if an object is connected to electricity. Some believe these photographs display an aura.

Knocks and Taps: This falls into the category of sound anomalies and has been used by investigators since the advent of time to establish communication. Also used by mediums to defraud the anguished and the lonely.

Langley, Jan: Paranormal expert, author of *Haunted Ghost Tours of Michigan's Upper Peninsula*, as well as many others. UPST affiliate. www.exploringthenorth.com/Michigan/Ghosts.html. 6. 180.

Lapalm, Gerry: UPST Certified Investigator.

Laser Grid: Devices that generate laser beams. When used in static or mobile fashion they illuminate shadows and manifestations. 79.

Appendix IV Glossarex

Lawrence, Bryson: UPST Certified Investigator and leader. One of the UPST Generals. Apt to accept the lock down when Uncle David is absent. 5, 8, 16, 40, 71, 114, 122, 124, C10 – 15, P5, P8, P104, P138, P170, P174, P188, P209, P238. P271.

Lawrence, Christian: UPST Certified Investigator and one of the UPST Generals. Has been called the most experienced investigator of his age in North America. V, 4, 26, 31, 40, 54, 68, 82, 100, 114, 122, 168, 178, 190, 204, 236, 272, C10-15, P4, P7, P8, P27, P28, P29, P31-P34, P38, P39, P40, P41, P50, P55, P68, P86, P87, P102, P104, P106, P110, P112, P122, P130, P138, P157, P160, P162 P168, P178, P188, P190, P204, P209, P212, P216, P225, P236, P238.

Lawrence, David: Founder of the UPST recognized by pink shorts and the moniker "The Old Man." 2, 237, 272, C10-15, P7, P8, P34, P41, P104, P107, P138, P143, P150, P188, P190, P194, P204, P211, P212, P225, P238. P271, P274.

Lawrence, Devin: UPST member and noted computer geek. Brother of David and Father of Rylie, Teagan and Gabriel. 3, 47, P47.

Lawrence, Gabriel: UPST Certified Investigator and IIT. 236, P87.

Lawrence, Rudoph: (Rudy) is a UPST member and ex-educator. He investigates occasionally but always has input as the Patriarch of the Lawrence clan. 3, 32, C11.

Lawrence, Rylie: UPST Certified Investigator. 114, 236, P7, P87, P104, P113, P122.

Lawrence, Teagan: UPST Certified Investigator.236, P39, P87, P122.

Leduc, Joseph: UPST Certified Investigator. "Joe" trains animals and is considered one of the Lawrence family. V, 5, 40, 71, 86, 109, 122, C10-C15, P41, P134, P135, P174, P178, P184, P188, P271.

Levitation: A physical object raising or floating in defiance of the law of gravity.

Life Review: Usually associated with near-death experiences when one's life flashes before their eyes.

Lights Out: As outlined previously, investigations are typically in the dark to avoid daytime noise, contamination of evidence, more thrills and chills, etc. The UPST calls this *Dead Time* or *Spook On*.

List, Mark: UPST Certified Investigator, USA veteran and chauffer. P23, P238.

Lockdown: This activity is a solo investigation in a hot or active spot at a location. 77, 141-147, 153, 160, 186, 190, P142, P143.

Lucid Dreaming: Where the dreamer is between consciousness and sleep but can recognize this fact enough to control the dream events.

Lustila, Betty: UPST Certified Investigator, researcher and cousin of the family Lawrence. 100, 116, 151, C10-C15, P20, P27, P46, P100, P101, P112, P188, P211, P271.

Magic: Sometimes called sorcery or conjuring is the practice or art of controlling or forecasting natural events, effects or forces by invoking the supernatural.

Mallus Malificarum: In English *The Hammer of Witches*, published in 1487 by two Catholic Priests of the Dominican Order became the instruction guide for future witch hunts.

Manifestation: The materialized form of a spirit or entity. See also: Chapter 2, *In Search of?*

Masters, Gregg: UPST Certified Investigator and USA veteran. 168, 272, P101, P168, P272.

Matrixing: Primarily visual but is also used to describe what the human mind does to fill in the gaps of any sense by constructing understandable results. See also: Pareidolia.

Mayan Calendar: A non-repeating calendar with sequences of about 400 years and the 13th ending on December 21, 2012. The basis for the doomsday predictions. Whew!

Medium: A person (usually a psychic) who claims to possess the ability to channel a spirit by allowing the deceased to speak or write messages using the medium's body on behalf of the living. 30, 47, 48, 97, 195.

Mesmerism: Or medium-mesmerism is a hypnotic sleep or trance state entered into by the medium or a subject. See also: Hypnotism.

Metaphysics: The division of philosophy that seeks to explain the primary nature of ultimate reality. Through exclusion modern theory includes things beyond immediate understanding.

Michigan Dog Man: An apparent animal sighted in the Upper Peninsula and parts of Wisconsin. Some believe a combination of man and wolf walking bipedal.

Miller, Jeff: UPST Certified Investigator, engineer and skeptic. 227, 231.

Miller, Lisa: UPST Certified Investigator, Mother, cook and ace photographer. Lisa captures anomalies on camera at every hunt. 22, 227, 231, 233, P7, P21, P99, P233, P238.

Appendix IV Glossarex

Miller, Shania: UPST Certified Investigator and daughter of Jeff and Lisa. 227. P7, P99, P238.

Miller, Tia: UPST member now hunts life. C13, 15, P182, P188, P271.

Milligauss: The unit of measurement that rates the strength of electro magnetic fields.

Mist: An anomaly that appears as a blanket of luminescent fog, usually photographed. 18, 60, P18.

Mitchell, David: UPST Certified Investigator and past owner of the Delft Theatre in Escanaba, MI. Husband of Rachel. P1, P238.

Mitchell, Rachel: UPST Certified Investigator and past owner of the Delft Theatre in Escanaba, MI. Wife of David. P238.

Morrison, Maggie: UPST Certified Investigator and niece (in hiding) of David Lawrence. P1, P15, P238.

Morrison, Shayna: UPST Certified Investigator and much to her chagrin, niece of David Lawrence. P1, P15, P238.

Motion Sensor: A device that produces infrared waves that, when broken, sound an alarm. 80.

Motor Automatism: Muscular movement not consciously controlled. See also: Automatic Writing.

Myers, Rich: Representative of the UPBFSO (Upper Peninsula Bigfoot Sasquatch Organization) member of the national BFRO (Bigfoot Research Organization) and UPST affiliate.

Nahma Inn: Located on the north side of Lake Michigan, this Michigan historical site offers paranormal activity along with great food, libations and lodging. 6, C14, P5, P21,

Nanteos Cup: An olivewood cup or bowl secreted in Britain during the reformation. Legend has it that this is the "Holy Grail." Strange healing activity surrounds the cup.

Nazca Lines: Ancient and gigantic images carved into the earth of figures like a man with a club to animals in the Nazca Valley of southern Peru and only visible from the air.

Near Death Experience: (NDE) is an experience that is reported by people who clinically die, or come close to death and are revived. Often accompanied by a bright white light.

Necromancy: The ability to communicate or resurrect the dead.

Necronomicon: The book of the dead. A collection of incantations said to open a doorway to the underworld and the unleashing of the ancient dead.

Nelson, George: 1908-1934. Born Lester Joseph Gillis and better known as "Baby Face Nelson." Gangster, bank robber & murderer. C11.

Newbie: An Investigator that has been schooled but is in training. 45, 47, 52, 69, 104, 214. See also: IIT.

Nexus: A means of connection, link or tie. In the paranormal it is the connection of the body to the spirit.

Night-Vision: An infrared device (usually goggles) that illuminate a visual spectrum allowing one to see with no light. See also: Infrared. 74, 84, 93, 94, 109, P93.

Nosferatu: Slavic term referring to a vampire or the "undead."

Obelisk: Basically a tool that offers pre-programmed responses to audio signals (your voice). This piece of equipment can fall anywhere from creepy to stupid. 94, C15, P94.

Occult: Generally referring to magical, mystical, experimental or satanic studies. Literally to mean concealed or hidden knowledge beyond pure reason and the physical sciences.

Old Hag Syndrome: A nocturnal phenomenon that involves a feeling of immobilization, suffocation and fear. See also: Sleep Paralysis, Crone.

Olson, Melissa: UPST certified member and leader of affiliate ICPI (Iron County Paranormal Investigation). 86, 121, C14, C15, P29, P41, P86, P193, P227.

Oppression: Feelings of angst, depression and foreboding often associated with malevolent entities. Some believe it a pre-condition of possession. 13, 15, 19, 20, 21, 23, 200. See also: Possession.

Orb: Literally a sphere or ball of light. Many believe that orbs can indicate the partial manifestation of any category of spirit. Most often caught on camera. 12, 21, 22, 23, 60, 61, 100, 146, 147, 174, P21.

Ouija Board: Also called a talking or spirit board. Some believe its name comes the French and German words for "yes," this is unlikely due to recent developments in the history of its Trademark. Many investigators refuse to use and even warn against their use.

Out-of-body experience: (OBE). When a person's consciousness exits the restrictions of the physical body. See also: Near Death Experience (NDE), Astral, Astral Plane and Astral Projection.

Parabolic Listening Device: A reverse cone-like structure that amplifies sound. This includes audio not heard by the human ear. 91. P91.

Appendix IV Glossarex

Paranormal: Referring to anything outside or beyond current scientific explanation. All subjects supernatural from spirit study to UFO's and Bigfoot.

Paranormal Activity: Incidents or occurrences at a location out of the normal realm.

Paranormal Research: The study of the paranormal. See also: Paranormal.

Paranormal Tourism: A facet of the travel industry catering to tourists that will attend paranormal conventions, pay to investigate famously haunted locations, take ghost tours, etc. The UPST attempts to steer clear of these spots.

Parapsychology: The study of mental abilities outside the practice of normal attributes or psychology.

Pareidolia: A psychological occurrence where random sensory stimulus is arranged into recognizable patterns. Sometimes called Matrixing. See also: Matrixing.

Parsons, Mike: UPST Certified Investigator. P238.

Past life regression: This therapy relies on a belief in reincarnation. Used by some hypnotherapists to try to get clients to remember their past lives. See also: Reincarnation.

Paulding Light: Near Watersmeet, MI. in Paulding. A mysterious light appearing every night at a distance from atop a steep grade. Legend speculates causes from a dead railroad brakeman to spirit wolves to faeries. Some continue touting a car light theory which has been debunked dozens of times. Also believed a portal. See also: Ghost Light, Portal, Vortex. VIII, 6, 21, 22, 26, 52, 53, 63, 72, 82, 87, 89, 90, 112, 113, 157, viii, P21, P41, P53, P55, P86, P112.

Peer Review: The findings of research evaluated by "peers." The concept of offering an alternate explanation or consideration on the merit of a study. Unfortunately, academics have used this notion to cut down new and creative ideology for centuries.

Pendulum: A weight at the end of a chain or cord that swings to and fro. In the paranormal the movement of the weight can be used to detect areas of paranormal energy, answers to questions, etc.

Phantom Animals: There is a belief that some spirits can take the form of animals rather than humans but it may also be the caring spirit of a beloved pet. This is activity is usually residual as in lying beside a fire, moving a dog bowl, etc. See also: Zoomorphism and Hell Hound.

Phasing: The practice of shuttling your camera in and out of infrared mode; usually in subdued lighting. This practice is in an attempt to catch objects that may be invisible to either the infrared or ambient visual spectrums. 84.

Polequin, Albert: (Al). UPST Certified Investigator and husband of Jenny. C15, P7, P113, P229, P274.

Polequin, Jenny: UPST Certified Investigator. C15, P113, P274.

Poltergeist: Taken from the German term for "noisy ghost," the poltergeist is a rare entity demonstrative of kinetic activity and loud noise designed to frighten. 13-14.

Portal: A theoretical doorway, entrance, or gate between two worlds, the physical and the spiritual. See also: Vortex.

Possession: The inhabitation by an entity of an oftentimes unwilling host where an exertion of control takes place. Most religions consider this demonic or evil in nature. 15.

Possessed Objects: Items that change appearance, move, make noise or create activity. Often associated with the spirit of a deceased person that owned or had possession of them.

Prayer: A meditative communication primarily with God, some believe a deity or spirit.

Precognition: Sensing or perceiving knowledge of the future. See also: ESP.

Pre-Hunt: Pre-Hunt Interview or preliminary hunt interviews are the first contact with the owners or trustees of a haunted location. It is an effort to gather information and history of all activity at a particular site.

Premonition: An intuition or psychic awareness of future events; good and bad.

Preternatural: Applies to things that are of the natural world but currently unexplained. The Loch Ness Monster and Sasquatch are among these (until the recent explainers of zero Bigfoot evidence have made the assertion that Sasquatch can jump dimensions☺).

Price, Harry: The first Ghost Hunter implementing scientific method and the technology of the time in an effort to prove the existence of an afterlife and to debunk frauds.

Primary Readings: Baseline measurements of energy readings at a haunted location used for establishing an investigation's course. See also: Baseline.

Appendix IV Glossarex

Projection: The ability to manifest an apparition with one's own conscious or non-conscious being.

Protection: Rites and rituals that guard human's from psychic and, or demonic intrusion.

Provocation: or provoking is the act of irritating or challenging a spirit in an effort to elicit a response. 13.

Psionics: (Psi) A practice that measures ESP using physical tools.

Psychic: A person who displays an extraordinary attunement to things outside normal existence and typically connected to the living and manifested at a young age, usually disappearing unless nurtured. Many fakes. 29, 30, 32, 48-49, 95, 120, 195, 202-203.

Psychic Impression: An image, history or an event received through precognition. See also: Precognition, ESP.

Psychokinesis: Also psycho kinesis or PK. The ability to use the mind to move an object. Some believe it can be an aspect in many hauntings; primarily in Poltergeist activity.

Quabbala: Also Cabbala or Kabbala. A Jewish mysticism which was the basis of an underground cult during the middle ages. Madonna practices it now. See: Derrrr.

Qualifications: There are no qualifications needed to be a paranormal investigator. Some, like popular television shows have began organizations that the UPST would have to diminish their standards to join. Read this book and do good work.

Rat Monkey: Established inhabitant of Sumatra, the offspring of a large shipboard rat raping the gentle monkeys of this poor African country. See also: Liberal Economics.

Raymond, Audrey: UPST Certified Investigator and co-leader of the Kid's Academies with Christian Lawrence. C14, C15, P229.

Raymond, Brenda: UPST Certified Investigator, researcher and executive secretary. 116, C14, C15, P25, P46, P232.

Raymond, Craig: UPST Certified Investigator and musician. C14, C15, P229.

Real Time Recorder: Audio recorder that employs a time buffer allowing nearly instant review of EVP. 17, 76.

Reciprocal Apparition: Picture Sixth Sense where a living person is able to communicate one on one with a spirit. Very, very rare.

Recorder: See: Audio Recorder.

Reincarnation: Many religions hold the belief that souls can be born again. According to this ideology, personalities may change but the core essence remains; perhaps to right past wrongs.

Religion: The belief and reverence for a supernatural all knowing power. Practices involved include adherence to written scripture and the study of a historical tradition.

Remote Viewing: Actually studied by the US government, this procedure allows a sensitive to enter a dream state seeing events, people, and locations at distance. See also: Sensitive, Astral Plane.

Reno, Mike: UPST Certified Investigator. P69. P238.

Report: When a case is concluded, applicable materials are posted (including video and other evidence). After analysis from the complete team, a report is issued summarizing the investigation.

Residual energy: Most experienced investigators adhere to the idea that acts of extreme human emotion, such as violence or death can leave an imprint on the tapestry of time. It is also thought repetitive activity can tear this fabric of the physical. 11, 12, 16, 17, 129, C2.

Residual Haunting: Repetitive activity resulting from an energy imprint of an event in time. These are demonstrative of residual energy and seem to replay like a tape loop. This does not include Intelligent Spirits or Active Haunts. See also: Residual Spirit, C2.

Retro cognition: Recognizing events from the past through a perception beyond the physical realm. Usually events the seer has no knowledge of.

Reveal: A discussion or presentation with the owner of an investigated location regarding the results of the hunt.

Ritual: The words or actions of a ceremony performed for their symbolic nature as prescribed by religion or tradition.

Riverside Cemetery: Germfask, Michigan and the home of the Lawrence family. Always active. V, 6, 97, PV, PP6,

Ryan, Coby: UPST Certified Investigator absent but with good reason; attending Harvard University. P11.

Sacrament: Formal Christian rite listed as one of those that must be gained to ascend.

Sacred: Holy practice or item declared holy set aside for worship of a deity. The state of being holy or sacred. Set apart for the worship or service of God or gods.

Satan: Adversary, Devil. Many religions relate this term to a demon or a fallen angel, minor god and idolatry, or as the epitome of evil.

Appendix IV Glossarex

Schwegel, Yvonne: (Vonnie).UPST member, and Aunt of Betty Lustila. P102.

Scientific Method: The scientific method collects information through observation, experimentation and the testing of the hypothesis. In paranormal study it boils down to DEBUNK everything and study the rest. 49.

Séance: A meeting of individuals in an attempt to communicate with the dead. Houdini denounced séances and exposed many as hoaxes in the late 19th and early 20th centuries. See also: Houdini.

Sedamsville Rectory: A deserted Catholic rectory and sanctuary in Cincinnati, Ohio. 190.

Sensitive: A person attuned to activity or events outside normal perception. Most people have a degree of sensitivity and almost all women believe they do.

Session: A pre-arranged time period for a squad at a particular location or room where they conduct an investigation. See also: Swing, Vigil.

Setup: After the team arrives, the setup begins. Equipment location, grids and DVR surveillance are placed as well as HQ, chargers, extra batteries, etc. See also: Grid.

Seul Choix Pointe Lighthouse: Finished in 1895, this Michigan historical landmark is recognized as the most haunted lighthouse on the Great Lakes. 4, 6, 8, 17, 40, 82, 89, 97, 273, C10, P8, P4, P40.

Shadow Figure: Is also called a Shadow Person or Shadow Ghost and in the pejorative; Black Masses. Shadow figures are partially manifested apparitions seen on investigations that most often appear in corners and out of the peripheral vision of the eye. They can also be indicative of an energy drain in a particular location which is also consistent with spiritual manifestation. 18, 84, 148, 149, 157, 168, 178, 233.

Simulcra: Along with matrixing and pariedolia this term is used to describe seeing everyday figures, faces and recognizable images in natural surroundings.

Sleep paralysis: An unusual catatonic state that occurs while going in or out of the sleep state. See also: Hypnagogia, Lucid Dreaming, Old Hag Syndrome, Crone.

Smudging: A ceremonial bundle of dried herbs, most commonly white sage sometimes rubbed or burnt in cleansings at an active location to alleviate spirits.

Soul: According to many religions is the inner-self unique to any living being.

Sparkles: Photographic visual effect that mocks a declining fireworks display.

Specialty Tool: Or item is a device intrinsic to or designed for the hunt that melds with history or the entity present. 81-82.

Specter: A ghostly apparition; a phantom. See also: Spirit, Ghost.

Spike: The sudden rise of a paranormal tool, such as an EMF detector, causing it to display heightened activity or signal.

Spirit: Usually the soul of a deceased. Some believe that "ghosts" exist in a suspension of disbelief not knowing they are dead. Others believe ghosts and spirits identical. See also: Cross Over.

Spirit Box: The device believed to allow contact with spirits through the use of a radio frequency. See also: Frank's Box, Ghost Box. 88, P88.

Spirit Guides: Mediums and spirituals use this term to describe an entity that aids them in providing communication between the dead and the living.

Spiritual healing: Use of religious or spiritual means in treating disease.

Spiritualism: A religious movement believing that spirits of the dead can be contacted by mediums and prominent between the 1840's and 1920's.

Spiritualists: Believing that some humans (mediums) can communicate with the dead and often through séances. Adhere to Spiritualism. See also: Spiritualism.

Spirituality: The practice of one's religious belief through study, practice and action.

Sprite: Defined as "elflike" and an elusive specter or ghost, is often thought akin to a fairy. See also: Faeries.

Squad: One of the fractions dividing a team for a hunt and usually from three to eight investigators.

Stafford, Kim: UPST Certified Investigator and ICPI member. C14.

Static Camera: Also called a Static Cam is an infrared video camera placed in key locations (Hot Spots) of an active location and allowed to run non-stop. 67, 80, 83, 84, 91, 107, C10-15.

Stigmata: The mysterious sores, bleeding, and marks on people in the same areas that Christ's wounds were placed during the crucifixion. First documented by St. Francis.

Appendix IV Glossarex

Supernatural: Anything existing outside the natural world. Usually referring to religious or spiritual matters. Laws of nature don't apply to this realm.

Surveillance: In paranormal research, an infrared DVR based system usually used for household or business protection. It is placed on an investigation to provide a comprehensive record of video (and sometimes audio). See also: Static Camera.

Swing: The UPST signal to shift to the next planned location on the grid. If activity is being monitored, extra time can be requested from the team leader. See also: Vigil, Session.

Synchronicity: Also called "the perfect storm." When a number of different factors combine to create circumstantial evidence which is beyond coincidence.

TAPs: 18. See also: Knocks and Taps.

Tarot Cards: A set of cards used by fortunetellers to help predict future events. This deck includes twenty two cards representative of love, death, fortune, etc.

Teams: The term that identifies the main group and sometimes the smaller groups that are broken into on an investigation. The UPST differentiates between the "team" as all members and "squads" with particular titles for the investigation.

Telekinesis: (Kinetic) The movement of objects by unknown means. This ability has been recorded on film most prevalently by Nina Kulagina of the Soviet Union. See also: Psychokinesis.

Telepathy: Communication from one mind to another without speech, visual means or ordinary sensory perception. See also: ESP.

Teleportation: A mode of transportation where matter or information is dematerialized in one location and reassembled in another. Teleportation has actually already been scientifically reproduced with light. (Beam us up Scotty).

Tesla Coil: Invented by Nikola Tesla in 1891 and creates electricity in the form of high voltage alternating current that may aid manifestation of spirits. 94.

Thanatology: The study of the death of human beings in all phases including pre-passing and post-death rituals.

Theology: The study of the nature of God, religions and the practice thereof.

Thermal Imager: High Tech, High Priced and controversial tool. 95.

Thought Form: A spiritual or metaphysical being projected by the power of the human mind. Also some believe that spirits are pure thought and manifest at will in the real realm. See also: Projection.

Thwack: A sound used by David Lawrence for audio anomalies. Described as the sound of a broomstick hitting the floor evenly.

Tibetan Book of the Dead: Or the Bardo Thodol is a text outlining the conscious experience of life after death before reincarnation.

Tool Kit: Screwdrivers, wrenches, batteries, battery chargers, checkers, etc. for hunt use. 98.

Trance: A detachment of one's physical self from their actual surroundings. Some believe the soul separates and can go elsewhere in this catatonic state. See also: Astral Plane, Remote Viewing.

Trans-Allegheny Lunatic Asylum: (Weston State Hospital) Built 1860-1864 (civil war held up construction). A Kirkbride design and the largest hand-cut stone building in America. 168.

TriField Meter: Detects three different forms of electro magnetic fields. 96.

Tripod: Three legged stand that can hold everything from a camera to a laser grid. A must have. 67.

Two-Way Radio: A electronic transmitter/receiver that allows instantaneous communication between squads sometimes over many miles. 70.

UFO: Unidentified Flying Object. By definition, any airborne object that does not fit known descriptions of existing aircraft. Commonly termed "flying saucer."

Unexplained: When insufficient evidence has been gathered to come to a conclusion.

Vigil: Used to describe an organized paranormal investigation where one location in a venue is studied for a period of time to search for signs of paranormal activity. See also: Session, Swing.

Voodoo: Also termed Hoodoo with slight variation. The mystical religion brought from Africa to the West Indies (Haiti) and still practiced to this day. 4, 150.

Vortex: Focused or concentrated spiritual energy accompanied by electro magnetic anomalies and increased paranormal activity. Some believe a vortex is a portal from one world to another, others a tear in dimensions. See also: Portal, Paulding Light, and Warp.

Wale, Frank: UPST Certified Investigator also known as Houdini because he always seems to disappear.

Appendix IV Glossarex

Walkthrough: The process of screening a haunted location before a hunt. The UPST advocates a pre-hunt walkthrough (interview) as well as a walkthrough with the team to set equipment and outline areas of concentration.

Warp: A location where the known laws of physics do not always apply and space/time may be distorted.

White Noise: A noise either natural or recorded of where volume is the same at all frequencies within a given band. 23, 75, 80, 85.

Wicca: The cult of witchcraft brought to public attention in 1954 after the British Witchcraft Act was repealed. Some few argue it a religion not totally based in paganism and sexual deviance.

Wind Meter: (Anemometer) detects wind speed and wind direction. Some believe that when a spirit manifests itself, a gust or breeze can be generated. 96.

Witch: A person that practices sorcery or is in league with the devil. Although typically feminine (witch), masculine equivalents include magician, wizard, sorcerer, and warlock. Modern day Wiccans have stolen the term in an effort to afford themselves a semblance of respect versus the deviance and bondage connections.

Witchcraft: The alleged exercise of supernatural or magical powers.

Wraith: The apparition of a living person. Sometimes wraith appearance coincides with the death of the person or a time of crisis.

Yaklyvich, Missie: UPST Certified Investigator. 82, C14.

Yeti: Also the Abominable Snow Man said to inhabit Tibet's Himalayan Mountains. Bipedal with human and apelike characteristics. See also: ABSM.

Zarcanor: An entity that asphyxiates or frightens people while they're asleep. Possibly Slavic or Scandinavian in origin. See also: Crone, Old Hag Syndrome.

Zener Cards: A set of printed cards used in testing ESP. Each contains five of the following cards: Five-pointed Star, Square, Cross, Circle, and Three Wavy Lines.

Zenith: The point on the celestial sphere directly above the observer. In paranormal, equivalent to the "nose on your face."

Zephyr: Insubstantial or passing on a western airstream. Some believe that spirits are carried upon and can manifest this wind.

Zippo: A past or random UPST member dismissed due to the incomprehension of team and/or family values. VIII, 5, 114,

Zombie: Term originating in Africa and then Haiti referring to the reanimated dead. The modern concept of "zombie" has become a cultural phenomenon not closely associated to the reality of the drug induced faux-death state that earned it the title. See also: Voodoo (Hoodoo).

Zoomorphism: An animal that presents attributes of a deity or demon.

Zupancic, Jason: UPST certified member, USA veteran and co-leader of affiliate ICPI (Iron County Paranormal Investigation). 121, C14, C15, P29, P227.

Stay in tune: www.upspookteam.info

"You think it's this one?" asked Gregg Masters.
Gregg drove his truck and I sat adjacent to him with Christian riding presidential.
We were hunting the little known RACO Airfield in Raco, Michigan. Gregg's being a veteran aided us in our identification of the many sites in this empty complex. With nearly six miles of airstrip, Raco is one of the largest deserted air force facilities in the nation. It was used during the cold war as a hidden station between K.I. Sawyer and Kinchloe Air force bases as well as a missile launch site.
"Yeah," I said, "I think this is the road."
At this point, we'd driven on Raco's spider web of two tracks surrounding the airfield for almost an hour.
"This has to be it," I added, "At least it runs north."
In addition to its miles of air strip and missile loading roadway, Raco also has a reputation for its countless UFO sightings. The UPST's Tania Belanger is also a MUFON (Midwest UFO Network) representative and has been called to Raco more than once.
"This has to be the road out," I spoke.
"I think we were here before," Christian chimed in,

Gregg Masters: Raco Air Strip Road Hunt

"I recognize that tree."
Somewhere in this huge Raco expanse, our UPST Gold Wing sat waiting for us.
"That's the road," I said.
I was wrong.

– RACO Air field, Raco, Michigan, 12:45 AM

272

Places to Visit

UPST - The Upper Peninsula Spook Team's Homepage. Hours of free video and join the team for unlimited access! Keep up on Christian's adventures.
www.UpSpookTeam.Info
www.facebook.com/UpSpookTeam

Seul Choix Pointe Lighthouse is known as the most haunted lighthouse on the Great Lakes. A must see!
www.exploringthenorth.com/SeulChoix/seul.html
www.facebook.com/SeulChoixPointLighthouse

The House of Ludington has a fabled history since the civil war. Kings, queens and Al Capone have called it home for at least a night.
www.HouseofLudington.com

The Helmer House Inn is a Michigan historic landsite and has not seen her better days.
www.michmarkers.com/startup.asp?startpage=L0981.html
www.facebook.com/pages/Helmer-House_Inn Historical-Marker/1392362661114071

The Jolly Inn is the iconic Yooper tavern. Let the Tovey's serve you some *Terrific* food and *Great* brew!
www.exploringthenorth.com/Jolly/Inn.html
www.facebook.com/ToveysJollyInn

The Nahma Inn is a beautiful bed & breakfast on Lake Michigan. *Great Food & Great Entertainment.* www.NahmaInn.com

Fayette Historic State Park may be unique in the entire world. A deserted town being re-furbished from building to building. A MUST for every historian's bucket list.
www.michigan.gov/mhc/0,4726,7-282-61080_62654---,00.html
www.uptravel.com/member-110/fayette-historic-townsite--state-parkfoot-trail-4706.html

---

Life is connected to death like meat to sinew; unavoidably cut but never totally severed. Order the steak rare!

CPSIA information can be obtained
at www.ICGtesting.com
Printed in the USA
LVOW13s0222131217
559572LV00029B/1940/P